IBC対訳ライブラリー

英語で読む
レ・ミゼラブル
Les Misérables

ヴィクトル・ユーゴー　原著
ニーナ・ウェグナー　英文リライト
平湊音　翻訳・英語解説

カバーイラスト＝Louis Léopold Boilly
ナレーション＝Greg Dale
録音スタジオ＝株式会社巧芸創作

本書の英語テキストは、弊社から刊行されたラダーシリーズ
『Les Misérables レ・ミゼラブル』から転載しています。

まえがき

　『レ・ミゼラブル』の作者、ヴィクトル・ユーゴー（1802-85）の生きた時代は、フランス革命（1789-99）が終わり、ナポレオン体制が崩壊した後の激動期にありました。

　いうまでもなく、フランス革命は王政を廃止し民衆が国家の主権者になろうとした事件です。1789年に革命が勃発して以来、90年にわたって、フランス社会は共和政治への模索の中で揺れることになります。

　ヴィクトル・ユーゴーが生まれたのは1802年。それは革命の混乱の中から台頭したナポレオン体制の真っ只中のことでした。その後皇帝になったナポレオンは、フランス革命に対抗するヨーロッパ諸国を制圧します。

　ヴィクトル・ユーゴーの父親ジョセフ・ユーゴーは、ナポレオンを信奉する有力な軍人でした。

　両親が不仲になったため、幼少期のヴィクトル・ユーゴーは母親に育てられたといわれています。やがて1815年にワーテルローの戦いでナポレオンが没落すると、フランスは列強によって革命前の体制に戻され、ルイ18世が王位につきます。

　それに伴って、彼の父親も失脚しますが、父親はその後もナポレオン体制の復活を望む「ボナパリスト」であったといわれています。

　1830年にルイ18世の後を継いだシャルル10世が7月革命で失脚します。『レ・ミゼラブル』はナポレオンが没落した頃からこの7月革命に至るフランスを舞台に描いたヴィクトル・ユーゴーの代表作なのです。

　詩人としても作家としても大成功を収めたヴィクトル・ユーゴーは、その後政界にも進出し、7月革命で為政者となったルイ・フィリップ政権の

中で、フランス革命以来の民主化運動を支えてゆきます。私生活では華や
かな女性関係など、スキャンダルに見舞われることも多かったといわれて
います。

　その後、ルイ・フィリップは富裕層と貧困層、そして労働者層との確執
から1848年に勃発した2月革命で政権の座を追われます。その後ナポレオ
ンの甥にあたる、ルイ・ナポレオンがクーデターを起こしナポレオン3世
として皇帝となると、ヴィクトル・ユーゴーは民主化運動の立場からそれ
を弾劾し、ベルギーへの亡命を余儀なくされます。

　『レ・ミゼラブル』は、そんな亡命生活の中で1862年に発表されます。こ
の作品の中には、彼の幼少期から28歳に至る頃のこうしたフランスの社会
状況が見事に描かれ、彼自身の体験も題材として取り込まれているのです。

　ヴィクトル・ユーゴーがパリに戻ったのは、ナポレオン3世がプロシア
との戦いに敗れ、政権の座を追われた1870年。そして他界したのは1885
年でした。それはフランスが第三共和政を樹立した5年後のことでした。
　彼は、フランス革命から第三共和政に至る動乱期を生きた作家だったの
です。そしてこの時期のフランスにはロシアに抑圧されたポーランドから
パリに移住したショパンなど、様々な芸術家が活躍していました。ヴィク
トル・ユーゴーは、そうした芸術の街、そして民主主義運動の震源地とも
なったパリを生きた人物でもあったのです。

　この小説を経て、こうした世界史の重要な舞台となったフランスのあら
ましを肌で感じていただければ幸いです。

IBC編集部

もくじ

Part I:
Fantine 11
ファンティーヌ
確かな読解のための英語表現 46

Part II:
Cosette 49
コゼット
確かな読解のための英語表現 68

Part III:
Marius 71
マリウス
確かな読解のための英語表現 110

Part IV:
The Rue Plumet 113
プリュメ街
確かな読解のための英語表現 170

Part V:
Jean Valjean 173
ジャン・ヴァルジャン
確かな読解のための英語表現 236

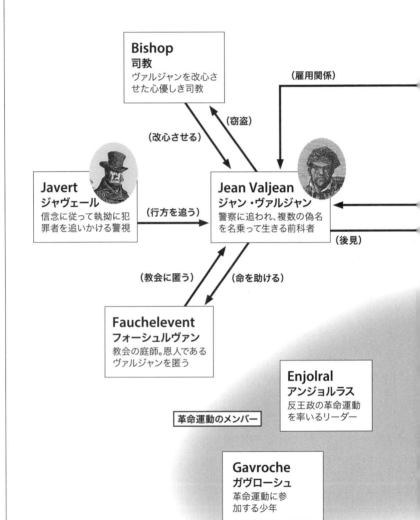

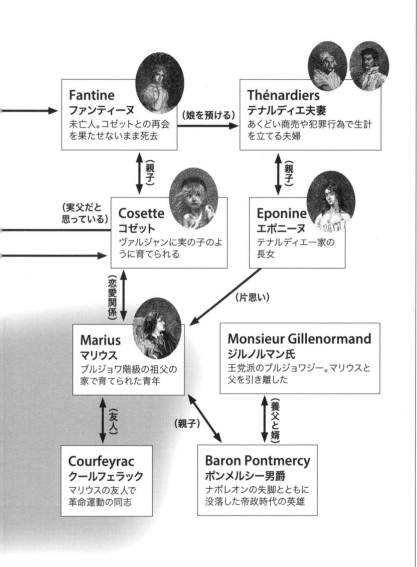

本書の構成

本書は、

□ 英日対訳による本文　　□ 欄外の語注
□ 確かな読解のための英語表現　　□ MP3形式の英文音声

で構成されています。

　本書は、フランスの作家ヴィクトル・ユーゴー原作の『レ・ミゼラブル』をや
さしい英語で書きあらためた本文に、日本語訳をつけました。

　各ページの下部には、英語を読み進める上で助けとなるよう単語・熟語の意
味が掲載されています。また英日の段落のはじまりが対応していますので、日
本語を読んで英語を確認するという読み方もスムーズにできるようになって
います。またストーリーの途中に英語解説がありますので、本文を楽しみなが
ら、英語の使い方などをチェックしていただくのに最適です。

付属のCD-ROMについて

**本書に付属のCD-ROMに収録されている音声は、パソコンや携帯音楽プレーヤーな
どで再生することができるMP3ファイル形式です。一般的な音楽CDプレーヤーでは
再生できませんので、ご注意ください。**

■音声ファイルについて

　付属のCD-ROMには、本書の英語パートの朗読音声が収録されています。本文左ペー
ジに出てくるヘッドホンマーク内の数字とファイル名の数字がそれぞれ対応しています。

　パソコンや携帯プレーヤーで、お好きな箇所を繰り返し聴いていただくことで、発音の
チェックだけでなく、英語で物語を理解する力が自然に身に付きます。

■音声ファイルの利用方法について

　CD-ROMをパソコンのCD/DVDドライブに入れて、iTunesなどの音楽再生（管理）ソ
フトにCD-ROM上の音声ファイルを取り込んでご利用ください。

■パソコンの音楽再生ソフトへの取り込みについて

　パソコンにMP3形式の音声ファイルを再生できるアプリケーションがインストールされ
ていることをご確認ください。

　CD-ROMをパソコンのCD/DVDドライブに入れても、多くの場合音楽再生ソフトは自
動的に起動しません。ご自分でアプリケーションを直接起動して、「ファイル」メニュー
から「ライブラリに追加」したり、再生ソフトのウインドウ上にファイルをマウスでドラッグ
＆ドロップするなどして取り込んでください。

　音楽再生ソフトの詳しい操作方法や、携帯音楽プレーヤーへのファイルの転送方法につ
いては、ソフトやプレーヤーに付属のマニュアルで確認するか、アプリケーションの開発
元にお問い合わせください。

Les Misérables

Part I:
Fantine

ファンティーヌ

I

Just before sunset on an October evening in 1815, a ragged traveler entered a little town. The first place he went was city hall, but he soon came back out to the street. He tried to find lodgings at every inn, but they all turned him away. News and rumors travel fast in a small town. One innkeeper said to the traveler, "We know who you are! You went into city hall, and you showed them an ex-convict's papers! We can't keep a person like you here."

After searching for hours, the tired traveler gave up. Just as he was lying down in the cold street to rest, a kind woman spoke to him. She pointed to a door and told him to try there for something to eat and a place to sleep.

Without much hope, the traveler went to the house and knocked. A kind-looking man opened the door. The traveler did not know that this was the bishop of the town's church. The man welcomed him into his home, but the traveler was tired of pretending. As soon as he stepped inside, his desperation and frustration came out in a hostile outburst.

■come back out to ～へ舞い戻る ■turn ~ away ～を追い返す ■travel 動①旅をする ②（噂などが）伝わる ■ex-convict 名前科者 ■just as ～すると同時に ■bishop 名司教 ■come out in ～という状態で出てくる

12　Part I: Fantine

I

　1815年10月のある日、夕陽が沈むころ、みすぼらしい身なりの旅人が小さな町にたどり着いた。まず役場に向かったが、すぐに通りへと舞い戻った。宿を一軒一軒当たったものの、片っ端から断られる。小さな町では、噂はすぐに広まるものだ。ある宿の主人が旅人にこう言った。「お前のことは知ってるぞ！　役場に行って、前科者の書類を見せたな！　お前のような奴を泊めるわけにはいかん」

　部屋を求めて数時間さまよったあと、旅人は疲れ果て、ついに諦めた。冷たい路面に横たわって休もうとすると、親切な女性が旅人に話しかけた。ある家の扉を指さして、あそこで食事と部屋を頼んでごらんなさいと言うのだ。

　半ばあきらめつつ、旅人は家に向かい、戸を叩いた。親切そうな男が戸を開けた。旅人は、その男がこの町の教会の司教であることを知らなかった。男は旅人を家に迎え入れたが、旅人はもう、善人面をするのにうんざりしていた。家に足を踏み入れると、いら立ちがつのり、やけになってこう吠えたてたのだ。

"Will you really let me stay here?" the traveler demanded. "I am Jean Valjean, an ex-convict who was in jail for nineteen years. I was jailed when I was young because I stole a loaf of bread! We were hungry! My sister had seven little children, and I was trying to feed them! But they arrested me and sentenced me to five years as a galley slave at Toulons. I tried to escape four times and they added years to my sentence. I served a total of nineteen years. Now I'm a free man. Free! But no one will take me!"

Jean Valjean glared at the bishop, who was listening quietly.

"Now that you know who I am and where I come from, will you take me?"

The bishop motioned for the ragged traveler to sit down at his table.

"I will tell the maid to make your bed. Will you join me for supper?"

"What! You won't throw me out?" cried Jean Valjean. "You are a kind man. You're an innkeeper, aren't you?"

"I'm the priest at this church," said the bishop.

"Oh, sir, you are very good!" said Jean Valjean.

■let ~ stay ～を宿泊させる　■a loaf of ひとかたまりの～　■sentence ~ to ～に…
の刑を言い渡す　■serve 勤服役する　■now that 今や～だから　■throw ~ out ～
を追い出す

14　Part I: Fantine

「本当に俺を泊めるっていうのか」と旅人は問い詰めた。「俺はジャン・ヴァルジャン。19年間牢にいた前科者だ。若いとき、パンを一つ盗んで牢屋にぶち込まれた。俺たちは腹が減っていたんだ！ 姉には小さい子が7人もいたから、あいつらに食わせてやりたかったんだよ。でも、俺は捕まって、ツーロンで強制労働5年の刑を喰らった。4回脱走しようとして、そのたびに刑期が延びた。結局19年も臭い飯さ。でも今は自由だ。自由なんだ！ でも、誰も俺を相手にしてくれない！」

ジャン・ヴァルジャンは司教を睨みつけた。司教は黙って聞いていた。

「もう俺が何者で、どこから来たか分かっただろう。それでも俺のことを迎えてくれるのか」

司教はみすぼらしい身なりの旅人に対し、食卓に着くよう身振りで促した。

「ベッドの支度をするようメイドに言いましょう。ご一緒に夕食はいかがですか」

「なんだって！ 俺を追い出さないのか」とジャン・ヴァルジャンは叫んだ。「あんたは親切だな。宿屋じゃないのか」

「私はこの町の牧師です」と司教は答えた。

「それは、立派なことですな」とジャン・ヴァルジャンは言った。

ファンティーヌ　15

The maid brought soup, bread, and wine. Jean Valjean ate this meal as if he had never eaten such delicious food before.

"You have had a long, hard journey," said the bishop when Jean Valjean was done. "You are welcome to rest here for as long as you like."

The bishop showed him to a little guest bedroom. After giving Jean Valjean a candle and some fresh water and towels to wash with, the bishop said good night.

Jean Valjean lay down on the bed. It felt like the most comfortable bed he had ever been in. However, he could not sleep. Jean Valjean was astounded at the kindness of the bishop, but he was troubled by his own future. After this night, he didn't know what he would do. He had to make a life for himself, but how?

Jean Valjean had always been a clever man, but nineteen years in jail made him hard and twisted. Imprisonment and mistreatment had turned his cleverness into cunning. He was only a desperate man when he went into jail, but he had come out a criminal.

■as if まるで~のように　■as long as you like 好きなだけずっと　■lie down on ~ の上に横になる　■turn ~ into ~を…に変える　■desperate 形 自暴自棄の

16　Part I: Fantine

メイドがスープとパン、それにワインを運んできた。ジャン・ヴァルジャンは、こんなに美味しい食事を生まれて初めて食べたかのように貪りついた。

　ジャン・ヴァルジャンが食べ終わると、司教は「長く、つらい旅をしてきたのですね」と言った。「どうぞ、お好きなだけ我が家でお休みください」

　司教はジャン・ヴァルジャンを小さな客室へと案内した。ろうそくや水、手を拭くタオルを渡して、司教は「お休みなさい」と言った。

　ジャン・ヴァルジャンはベッドに横たわった。今まで、これほど心地のよいベッドに横たわったことはなかった。でも、眠れなかった。ジャン・ヴァルジャンは、親切きわまる司教に驚いてもいたが、同時に、自分の行く先も不安だった。今晩は助かった。でもこれからどうするのか、かいもく見当もつかない。自力で稼がなければいけないが、一体どうすればよいというのだ。

　ジャン・ヴァルジャンは生まれてこのかた頭のよい男だったが、19年も牢にいるうちに、かたくなで、ひねくれた心の持ち主になっていた。牢屋でひどい仕打ちを受けるうちに、賢さが狡猾さに変わっていた。牢に入ったときはただのやけっぱちな男だったが、いつしか身も心も盗人になってしまったのだ。

ファンティーヌ　17

Silently, Jean Valjean got out of bed. He had seen a cupboard full of silver plates in the room where he had eaten. He put on his clothes and stepped out of his room. The whole house was quiet. Jean Valjean felt a pang of guilt for what he was about to do. After all, the bishop had been so kind! He had treated Jean Valjean like a man, and an equal! But Jean Valjean felt he had no choice. He straightened, went to the cupboard, took the silver, and disappeared into the darkness.

The next morning, the bishop heard a knock at his door. There were three policemen there, holding a wretched-looking man. It was the traveler from the night before.

"Sir, we have reason to believe that this thief robbed your house last night!" said one of the policemen. "See here? In his bag he carries silver stamped with the sign of your church!"

"Ah!" cried the bishop. "Jean Valjean, there you are! I'm glad to see you. Look here, you forgot the candlesticks that I gave you! Why did you not take them along with the silver plates? Please, gentlemen, let him go."

Jean Valjean stared at the bishop in shock.

■put on 〜を着る　■step out of 〜の外に出る　■pang of 〜による苦しみ　■after all あれほど〜なのに　■have reason to believe 〜を信じるだけの根拠がある　■stamp 動 〜を刻印する　■along with 〜と一緒に

18　Part I: Fantine

ジャン・ヴァルジャンは、そっとベッドを抜け出した。食事をした部屋で、銀の皿でいっぱいの食器戸棚を目にしていたのだ。服を着て、部屋から出た。家じゅうが静まり返っている。ジャン・ヴァルジャンは、これからやろうとしていることに良心の呵責を覚えた。なぜかって、司教はあれほど親切だったのに！　司教は、ジャン・ヴァルジャンを人間として、それも同じ人間として迎えてくれた。でも、ジャン・ヴァルジャンには、もうほかになす術はなかった。背筋を伸ばして食器戸棚に向かい、銀の皿を取って、夜の闇へと消えたのである。

　翌朝、司教は自宅の戸をノックする音を耳にした。三人の警官が哀れな男を取り押さえている。見ると、昨晩の旅人だった。

　「司教様、この盗人が昨晩お宅で盗みを働いたはずです」と警官の一人が言った。「こちらをご覧ください。こいつのかばんに、教会の刻印の入った銀食器が入っておりました！」
　「ああ」と司教は大声で言った。「ジャン・ヴァルジャン。そこにいらしたんですね。お会いできて良かった。ご覧なさい、燭台も差し上げたのに、お忘れですよ。なぜ銀の皿と一緒にお持ちにならなかったのですか。みなさん、どうぞヴァルジャンさんを放してあげてください」
　ジャン・ヴァルジャンは、驚きのあまり司教をぽかんと見つめていた。

ファンティーヌ　19

"You mean to say you know this man?" asked a policeman. "And he did not steal from you?"

"Yes, I know him. This silver was a gift. Let him go."

Bewildered, but believing the priest, the police let Jean Valjean go.

With tears welling up in his eyes, Jean Valjean continued to stare at the priest.

"My friend," said the priest, "before you go away, here are the candlesticks. Take them."

Jean Valjean was shaking. He took the candlesticks silently.

"Now, go in peace. And if you should ever come here again, you are always welcome. The door is always open, day and night."

Jean Valjean dropped his head in gratitude and shame.

"Just promise me," said the bishop, "that you will use this silver to become an honest man."

■mean to 〜するつもりである　■bewildered 形面くらった、困惑した　■well up 湧き上がる　■go in peace ごきげんよう　■if ~ should ever もし〜が…することがあればいつでも　■drop one's head うなだれる

「この男とはお知り合いということですか」と警官はたずねた。「あなたの物を盗んだわけではないのですね」

「ええ。この方のことは存じ上げています。この銀食器は差し上げたものです。どうぞ解放してあげてください」

面くらいつつも、司教の言葉を信じた警察はジャン・ヴァルジャンを解放した。

目に涙をたたえながら、ジャン・ヴァルジャンは司教を見つめ続けた。

「友よ」と司教は言った。「行かれる前に、こちらの燭台をお持ちください」

ジャン・ヴァルジャンは震えていた。彼は何も言わずに、燭台を受け取った。

「では、ごきげんよう。また我が家にいらっしゃることがあれば、いつでも歓迎しますよ。昼でも夜でも、扉は開いています」

感謝と恥じ入る気持ちが入り交じって、ジャン・ヴァルジャンは首を垂れた。

「一つ、約束していただけますか」と司教は言った。「この銀は、正直者になるために使うことを」

ファンティーヌ　21

II

A few years later, another traveler—a young woman—came across an inn in Montfermeil, a suburb of Paris. The woman's name was Fantine. She carried her daughter, a beautiful little girl about three years old. There were two children about the same age playing outside the inn. Their mother sat in the doorway, watching.

"What beautiful children," said Fantine to the woman. The two women began to talk.

"Is that your child?" the woman asked.

"Yes, her name is Cosette," said Fantine. "Your inn looks very comfortable."

"Do you want a room?"

"Well, no...But I wonder if you will do me another service. I am a widow. My husband died recently. I must support my child now, so I am traveling to my hometown of Montreuil-sur-Mer to find work. May I leave my child in your care? I have money to pay you every month, and it would be nice for her to have other children to play with."

■come across ふと〜を見つける ■about the same age 同じ年頃の ■wonder if 〜ではないかと思う ■widow 图未亡人 ■leave a child in someone's care 子供を(人)に預ける

II

　数年後、若い女性の旅人がパリ郊外のモンフェルメイユにある宿屋に
やってきた。ファンティーヌという名前の女性である。ファンティーヌは、
娘を連れていた。3歳ほどの、目鼻立ちの整ったかわいい女の子である。宿
の外では、ほぼ同い年の子供が二人遊んでいた。母親の女将が戸口に腰か
け、様子をうかがっている。

　「かわいいお子さんたちですこと」とファンティーヌは女将に話しかけ、
二人は話し始めた。
　「こちらはあなたのお子さんですか」と女将はたずねた。
　「ええ、コゼットといいます」とファンティーヌは答えた。「ここの宿は居
心地が良さそうですね」
　「お泊りですか」
　「いえ、泊まりはしないのですが、別のことをお願いできないかと思いま
して。私は未亡人で、先ごろ夫に先立たれました。これから子供の面倒を見
なければならないので、仕事を探しに故郷のモントルイユ=シュル=メー
ルに帰る途中なのです。そういうわけで、子供を預かっていただけないで
しょうか。毎月お支払いはいたします。娘にしても、ほかのお子さんが遊
び相手になってくれれば何よりですから」

ファンティーヌ　23

The woman narrowed her eyes and thought a moment.

"How much will you pay?"

"I can afford six francs a month."

"Seven," came a voice from inside the inn. A man appeared at the door behind the woman.

"I am Thénardier, and this is my wife. I own this inn. You'll need to pay seven francs a month, plus fifteen more right now for immediate expenses."

"I will pay it," said Fantine.

Fantine never knew what a mistake this was. She was only grateful for the Thénardiers' willingness to help. From that day on, Cosette lived with the Thénardiers, and for four years following, she never had a kind word from anyone. After Fantine left, the Thénardiers treated Cosette like a servant. The money that Fantine sent every month was used on everything but Cosette.

■can afford（支払いの）余裕がある ■right now 今すぐに ■from that day on その日以来 ■for ~ years following それから～年間 ■everything but ～以外のすべて

24   Part I: Fantine

女将は眉をひそめて、少し考えた。

「いくら払うの」

「月に６フランお支払いできます」

「７フランだ」と宿の中から声がした。女将の背後から男が戸口に現れた。

　「私はテナルディエ。こちらは妻。宿の主人は私だ。月々７フラン払いなさい。それと、当座の費用として、今すぐあと15フランだ」

　「お支払いします」とファンティーヌは言った。

　ファンティーヌは、ひどい過ちを犯したことに気づかなかった。テナルディエ一家が助けてくれるというので、感謝の念で一杯だったのだ。この日から、コゼットはテナルディエ一家の下で暮らすこととなった。それから４年間、コゼットは誰からも優しい言葉一つかけられることはなかった。ファンティーヌがいなくなると、テナルディエ家の人たちはコゼットを召使いのように扱った。ファンティーヌが毎月送ったお金がコゼットのために使われることは決してなかったのである。

ファンティーヌ　25

III

*I*n the town of Montreuil-sur-Mer, a man who nobody knew had arrived several years ago and had become a very successful businessman. He went by the name of Monsieur Madeleine. He invented a new clasp that revolutionized the manufacture of a popular type of bracelet. Eventually, he set up his own factory. He was successful, kind, and employed everyone who needed a job. He seemed to always think about others more than himself. He went to church every Sunday. He became very rich but always gave his money away, and he continued to live very simply. The only expensive thing he had in the room where he lived was a pair of silver candlesticks, which were displayed on his mantle.

■nobody knows 誰も知らない　■go by the name of ～と呼ばれている　■clasp 图 留め金　■set up ～を設立する　■give one's money away 金を分け与える

III

　数年前、見知らぬ男がモントルイユ＝シュル＝メールの町に現れ、事業で大成功を収めた。男はムッシュ・マドレーヌと名乗っていた。彼が発明した新しい留め金は、人気の型のブレスレットの作り方を一変させたのである。ついに、マドレーヌは自分の工場を設立した。彼は大成功を収めたばかりではなく、やさしく、仕事が必要な人を誰でも雇い入れた。いつも、自分のことではなく、他の人のことを考えているようだった。日曜日には毎週教会に行った。大金持ちになったのに、金をくれてやってばかりで、相変わらずつつましく暮らしていた。住んでいる部屋に置いてある金目の物は、炉棚の上に飾られている一対の銀の燭台だけだった。

ファンティーヌ　27

Monsieur Madeleine was so popular as an employer and a citizen that everyone in the town gradually came to respect and love him, all except one man. His name was Javert, and he was a police inspector. There is in some men the ability to recognize a beast, and he watched Madeleine with suspicious eyes always.

One day, in Montreuil-sur-Mer, a working man was caught under the wheels of his cart. It was old Fauchelevent, the gardener. Monsieur Madeleine was nearby as a crowd gathered. Seeing the old man under the cart, Monsieur Madeleine cried out, "I will give twenty luis to anyone who can lift this cart!"

Nobody stepped forward.

"Come, he is hurt! He may die! Thirty luis, then. Anyone?"

Javert, who was also among the crowd, was watching Madeleine with narrowed eyes.

"I only knew of one man who was strong enough to lift such a cart," said Javert. "He was a convict at Toulons."

■gradually come to だんだんと~するようになる ■all except ～を完全な例外として ■be caught under ～の下敷きになる ■cry out 叫ぶ ■step forward 名乗り出る

28   Part I: Fantine

ムッシュ・マドレーヌは、雇い主としても市民としても人気が高く、町の人たちはみな、だんだんと彼のことを敬愛するようになった。しかし一人だけ例外がいた。ジャヴェールという名の警視だ。けだものの心を見抜く力を備えた人がいるものだが、ジャヴェール警視はマドレーヌをいつも疑いの目で見ていた。

　ある日、モントルイユ＝シュル＝メールの町で、ある労働者が自分の荷車の車輪の下敷きになってしまった。庭師のフォーシュルヴァン爺である。やじ馬が集まる中、近くに居合わせていたムッシュ・マドレーヌは荷車に敷かれた老人を見て、「この荷車を持ち上げたら20ルイあげよう」と叫んだ。

　名乗りを上げる者はいなかった。

　「誰か！　この人はけがをしているんだ。死んでしまうぞ。30ルイだ。誰かいないか」

　群衆にまぎれていたジャヴェールは、いぶかしげにマドレーヌを見つめていた。

　「私は、こんな荷車を持ち上げられる力のある男を一人だけ知っていました」とジャヴェールは言った。「ツーロンの徒刑場の囚人だった男です」

ファンティーヌ　29

Monsieur Madeleine looked at Javert with startled eyes and seemed to shiver at this statement. But when he looked at the man suffering under the cart, he took off his coat. Madeleine put his broad back under the cart, and, straining with all his might, began to lift it. Others joined to help. They were finally able to get the cart off of Fauchelevent and saved his life. Throughout it all, Javert continued to stare at Madeleine with narrowed eyes.

■with startled eyes 驚いた目で　■take off ～を脱ぐ　■back 图背中　■with all one's might 力いっぱいに　■get ~ off ～を取り除く

ムッシュ・マドレーヌは驚いた目つきでジャヴェールを見つめた。彼の言葉を聞いて震えているようだった。しかし、荷車の下で苦しむ男を見るなり、マドレーヌはコートを脱いだ。マドレーヌは広い背中を荷車の下にすべり込ませ、力の限りを尽くして荷車を持ち上げ始めた。周りの人たちも加勢した。皆はついにフォーシュルヴァンを荷車から脱出させて、命を救ったのである。でも、ジャヴェールは終始、マドレーヌに疑いのまなざしを注ぎ続けていた。

ファンティーヌ　31

IV

In 1820, Monsieur Madeleine became the mayor of Montreuil-sur-Mer. Although he refused the request several times, the public wanted him, and he decided to take on the role of a civil servant. This same year, Fantine had left Cosette in Montfermeil with the Thénardiers and had come back to her hometown. She got a job at Mayor Madeleine's factory.

One morning several years later, Mayor Madeleine received a difficult request from Fantine, one of his best employees. She had been ill for about two months, and she was in the hospital. However, just as Mayor Madeleine was sitting down to write his reply to Fantine, Inspector Javert entered the office.

"Sir, I have come here to confess to a crime," said Javert stiffly. He stared straight ahead. "Once I confess, you must dismiss me from my position."

■mayor 图市長　■take on a role of ～の役割を担う　■civil servant 公務員
■write one's reply 返事を書く　■confess to a crime 罪を告白する　■stare straight ahead まっすぐ前を見る

IV

　1820年、ムッシュ・マドレーヌは、モントルイユ＝シュル＝メールの市長になった。マドレーヌは市長への就任要請を何度か断っていたのだが、市民たちはマドレーヌに市長になってほしいと願っており、マドレーヌはついに、市民の僕として市長となることを決心したのだ。同じ年に、ファンティーヌはモンフェルメイユのテナルディエ一家の下にコゼットを残し、生まれ故郷のモントルイユ＝シュル＝メールに戻ってきていた。ファンティーヌは、ムッシュ・マドレーヌの工場で働いていた。

　数年後のある朝、マドレーヌ市長は、ファンティーヌからやっかいな頼みごとをされていた。ファンティーヌは最高の働きをしていたが、ここ二か月ほど病に苦しんで入院していたのだ。しかし、マドレーヌ市長が腰かけてファンティーヌへの返事をしたためようとすると、ジャヴェール警視が市長室に入ってきた。

　「市長、私は罪を打ち明けにまいりました」とジャヴェールはぎこちなく言った。前をまっすぐ見つめていた。「自白が終わったら、私は解任されなければなりません」

ファンティーヌ　33

"What do you mean?" asked Madeleine.

"I—I denounced you, sir, to the chief of police in Paris," replied Javert. He faltered for a moment, but he regained his composure and stood very straight.

"What did you say to the chief? Surely, there is no reason for dismissal."

"I must be punished," continued Javert. He looked down now, looking ashamed. "I believed you were a convict. I thought I knew you from the galleys in Toulons, where I worked for many years. I thought you were Jean Valjean, who was released from the galleys in 1815. After his release, he robbed a bishop of a great amount of silver, and the authorities have been trying to catch him ever since."

The mayor turned pale.

"But now I know I was wrong, sir, for the real Jean Valjean has been caught. He faces trial tomorrow."

"Indeed?" replied Madeleine. It was all he could do to remain calm.

■denounce 剾告発する　■regain one's composure 落ち着きを取り戻す　■ever since その後ずっと　■turn pale 青ざめる　■face trial 裁判を受ける

「どういうことですか」とマドレーヌはたずねた。

「私は……私はあなたのことをパリ警察署長に告発したのです」とジャヴェールは答えた。一瞬ひるんだが気を取り直し、直立不動の姿勢を取った。

「署長に何と言ったのですか。解任されるいわれはありませんがね」

「私は罰を受けなければなりません」とジャヴェールは言った。今度はうつむいて、恥じているようだった。「あなたが罪人だと思っていたのです。ツーロンの徒刑場出身かと。というのも、ツーロンに長年勤めていたものですから、あなたの正体は、1815年に徒刑場から釈放されたジャン・ヴァルジャンだと思っていたのです。ジャン・ヴァルジャンは、司教から大量の銀を奪い取り、それから警察は奴の行方をずっと追っているのです」

市長は青ざめた。

「でも、私が間違っておりました。本物のジャン・ヴァルジャンが捕まり、明日裁判にかけられることになっているのです」

「本当ですか」とマドレーヌは答えた。平静を保つには、そうするしかなかったのだ。

ファンティーヌ　35

"Yes, sir. A man who goes by the name of Champmathieu who was arrested for stealing apples. When he was taken to jail, one of the prisoners recognized him as Jean Valjean, the convict at Toulons. Other prisoners who had been at Toulons recognized him too. Upon hearing this, I went to the jail to see him—and it is true! The man *is* Jean Valjean! He is much older now, but it's him. His trial is tomorrow and I will testify. But first I must apologize for denouncing you, and you must punish me."

Madeleine felt faint. He wanted Javert out of the room.

"Well, I'm very busy at the moment. Go to the trial, Javert, and we shall figure out how to deal with you later. Good day."

Javert left the room. Madeleine sat in silence, utterly shocked, but with a strange calmness coming over him. This man Champmathieu had been caught in a terrible misunderstanding. Jean Valjean could not possibly let another man go to jail for him. No, he would have to confess. There was no other way. This was what God wanted—he could not live this lie anymore.

■upon hearing this これを聞いて　■feel faint めまいがする　■figure out how to ～する方法を考える　■come over（急に）～に訪れる　■can not possibly とても～できない　■live a lie 偽りの生活を送る

36　Part I: Fantine

「ええ、そうです。シャンマティユーという通り名で、リンゴを盗んだかどで捕まった男です。牢に連れて行かれると、囚人の一人が、あれはツーロンで服役していたジャン・ヴァルジャンだと言い出しました。ツーロンで服役していた他の囚人たちも、奴の顔を知っていました。この話を聞いて、私も牢屋でその男の顔を見てまいりました。皆の言う通りでした。あの男はジャン・ヴァルジャンです！　ずいぶん年を取りましたが、間違いありません。明日裁判が開かれて、私も証言します。でもまず、あなたを告発したことを謝罪しなければなりません。そして、あなたは私を罰しなければならないのです」

　マドレーヌはめまいを感じ、ジャヴェールに部屋から出ていってもらおうと思った。

　「さて、私は今とても忙しいんです。ジャヴェールさん、裁判にお出かけください。そうすれば、あなたの処遇についてもはっきりするでしょう。ごきげんよう」

　ジャヴェールは部屋を去った。マドレーヌは一人静かにいすに腰掛けていた。ひどくショックを受けたが、不思議な静けさが身を包んでいた。このシャンマティユーという男は、あられもない誤解を受けている。自分の身代わりに他人を牢屋に行かせてはならない。自白するしかないだろう。他に道はない。これぞ神の思し召しだ。もう、偽りの生活を送るわけにはいかない。

ファンティーヌ　37

The next day, to everybody's surprise, Mayor Madeleine came to the trial of Champmathieu. The arrested man did indeed look very much like him, though a bit older. It was easy to see how someone could mistake him for Jean Valjean.

Madeleine had arrived just in time—Javert had already testified and left, and the judge was about to give his ruling. Madeleine interrupted the judge and called out for everyone in the courthouse to look at him.

"You all know me as Mayor Madeleine," he said, "but my real name is Jean Valjean. This man is innocent. Release him. I am the convict at Toulons who stole from the bishop. I belong in jail."

The entire courthouse was so shocked nobody made a sound.

"I will go home to make my preparations. You know where I live. You are welcome to come and arrest me."

With that, Jean Valjean walked out of the courthouse.

■to one's surprise 驚いたことに　■easy to see 容易に見て取れる　■just in time ぎりぎりの時間に　■call out 掛け声をあげる　■belong in jail 刑務所に入るのが相当である

翌日、マドレーヌ市長がシャンマティユーの裁判にやって来て、皆を
あっと驚かせた。逮捕された男はマドレーヌよりも少し年配だったが瓜二
つだった。シャンマティユーとジャン・ヴァルジャンを取り間違えたのも
無理はない。

　マドレーヌ市長は何とか間に合って到着した。ジャヴェールはすでに証
言を終えて退廷し、判事が判決を言い渡そうとしていたところだった。マ
ドレーヌは判事をさえぎり、法廷にいたすべての人に対し、自分に注目す
るようにと声を張り上げた。

　「皆さんは、私がマドレーヌ市長だと思っていることでしょう」と彼は
言った。「でも私の本名はジャン・ヴァルジャンです。この人は潔白です。
釈放してあげてください。私はツーロン徒刑場の囚人で、司教の財産を盗
みました。私は牢に入ります」

　法廷にいた人々は、衝撃のあまり物音一つ立てなかった。

　「私は自宅に戻って支度をします。私の家をご存じですね。どうぞ、私を
逮捕しにいらしてください」

　こう言い残して、ジャン・ヴァルジャンは法廷から出ていった。

ファンティーヌ　　39

V

Jean Valjean knew he had little time to make his preparations before he was arrested. First, he went to the bank and withdrew six-hundred thousand francs, his entire savings. He took this money home. It can be guessed that his intent was to give this money to the poor. Next, he headed to the hospital. One thing that weighed on his mind was the request of Fantine, his employee who was dying. He decided to pay her one last visit.

Jean Valjean arrived at the hospital to find Fantine lying in bed, pale and thin.

"Mayor Madeleine!" she said weakly when she saw him. "Do you have Cosette?"

This was the request Fantine had made—she had wanted Madeleine to bring back her child from Montfermeil.

■withdraw 動（預金を）引き出す ■head to ～へ向かう ■weigh on someone's mind 心に重くのしかかる ■pay ~ a visit ～を訪問する ■bring back ～を連れ戻す

40　Part I: Fantine

V

　ジャン・ヴァルジャンは、逮捕前に身辺を整理する時間が限られていることを自覚していた。まず、銀行に出かけて60万フランを下ろした。全貯金に相当する額である。彼は、この金を家に持ち帰った。貧しい人たちに与えるつもりで下ろしたのだろうと思われる。次に、病院へと向かった。ジャン・ヴァルジャンが気に病んでいたことの一つに、ファンティーヌの頼みがあった。息を引き取ろうとしている従業員である。そこで、最後にお見舞いに行くことにした。

　ジャン・ヴァルジャンは病院に赴き、ファンティーヌが横になっているのを見た。顔は青白くやせこけていた。
　「マドレーヌ市長！」ファンティーヌは彼を目にして弱々しく言った。「コゼットを連れていらしたのですか」
　これがファンティーヌの頼みだった。娘をモンフェルメイユから連れ戻してくれるようにと、マドレーヌに依頼していたのだ。

ファンティーヌ　41

Jean Valjean had not been able to go to Montfermeil because of the news Javert had brought him the day before. But he could not bear to disappoint Fantine.

"There now, you must rest," he told Fantine, taking her hand. "Your Cosette is well."

"Oh, you do have her then! When will I see her?"

Seeing the joy in Fantine's eyes, Jean Valjean's heart sank. It was impossible for him to get Cosette before he was arrested. He didn't have enough time. Before he could reply, the door burst open, and Javert strode into Fantine's room.

"Come along!" he yelled at Jean Valjean. His eyes gleamed with triumph, and he grabbed the mayor by the shoulder.

"What is happening, Mayor Madeleine?" asked Fantine, very frightened. "Why are the police here?"

"Inspector Javert," said Jean Valjean as quietly as he could, "you may arrest me, but I ask for just three days. Please, wait three days so I can go to Montfermeil to get this woman's child and place her in good care."

But it wasn't quiet enough—Fantine heard.

■can't bear to ～するのは忍びない　■there now さあさあ　■heart sinks 気落ちする　■burst open 弾けるように開く　■stride into 大股で～に入っていく　■come along こちらへ来い

前日にジャヴェールの知らせを聞いたため、ジャン・ヴァルジャンはモンフェルメイユに行くことができなかった。でも、ファンティーヌを気落ちさせるのは忍びなかった。

　「ここにいますよ、もう休まないといけません」と彼はファンティーヌに言い、手を取った。「あなたのコゼットは元気です」

　「ああ、それでは、あの子を連れ戻してくれたのですね。娘にはいつ会えますでしょうか」

　ファンティーヌの目に宿る喜びの光を見て、ジャン・ヴァルジャンの心は沈んだ。逮捕される前にコゼットを引き取るのは無理だ。時間がない。返事をする前に扉が荒々しく開き、ジャヴェールがファンティーヌの部屋につかつかと入ってきた。

　「こっちへ来い！」とジャヴェールはジャン・ヴァルジャンを怒鳴りつけた。勝ち誇ってらんらんと光る眼で、ジャヴェールは市長の肩をつかんだ。

　「どうされましたの、マドレーヌ市長」とおびえたファンティーヌはたずねた。「なぜここに警察がいるのです」

　「ジャヴェール警視、私を逮捕してもかまいませんが、三日間猶予をください」とジャン・ヴァルジャンはできるだけ小さな声で言った。「どうぞ三日間だけお待ちください。その間にモンフェルメイユに出かけて、この婦人のお子さんを引き取ってきちんと面倒を見てもらうようにしますから」

　でも、ファンティーヌに聞こえないほど小さい声ではなかった。

ファンティーヌ　43

"You do not have Cosette?" Fantine's pale face turned absolutely white. All her strength left her, and a single tear rolled down her face.

"I shall not see my child…"

She closed her eyes, and with one last breath, Fantine's head fell limply to the side. She was dead.

"Dear God!" cried Jean Valjean. He shook off Javert's hand and went to the dead woman. He said a prayer over her, straightened her body, and crossed her hands over her chest. Then he looked Javert straight in the eyes.

"Take me," he said.

■roll down 流れ落ちる　■fall limply to the side ガクッと一方に傾く　■Dear God! おお神よ！　■shake off 〜を振り払う　■say a prayer 祈りを捧げる

「コゼットを連れ戻していらっしゃらなかったのですね」ファンティーヌの青白い顔からは、生気が全くなくなった。一切の生気が消え去り、一粒の涙が顔を流れ落ちた。

「娘に会うことはできない運命なのね……」

ファンティーヌは目を閉じ、最後の息を吐いた。頭が力なく横を向いた。ファンティーヌは冥土に旅立ったのである。

「おお、神よ！」とジャン・ヴァルジャンは叫んだ。彼はジャヴェールの手を振り払い、息を引き取った婦人の下へと歩み寄った。ファンティーヌに祈りをささげ、身体をまっすぐにしてやり、胸の上で両手を組ませた。それからジャン・ヴァルジャンは、ジャヴェールの目をまっすぐ見つめた。

「連行するがよい」と彼は言った。

確かな読解のための英語表現 ［文法］

同 格

基本的な文法事項をきちんと押さえていると、英文の意味を確実に取ることができるため、読んでいてもくっきりと場面が浮かび上がってきます。楽しく英語の物語を読むために、学校文法を見直してみましょう。ここでは、語句に説明を加えたり、言い換えをするときに使う同格表現を取り上げます。

It was <u>old Fauchelevent</u>, <u>the gardener</u>. (p.28, 8行目)
庭師のフォーシュルヴァン爺である。

【解説】 この文で、old Fauchelevent という人物が初めて登場します。まず名前だけ出し、職業を次の the gardener で説明しています。このように、名詞や名詞句を、後から同じように名詞や名詞句で説明していく関係を、同格と言います。old Fauchelevent と the gardener はどちらも名詞であり、名詞同士の同格の場合、間にコンマが入っている文が多く見られます。

One morning several years later, Mayor Madeleine received a difficult request from <u>Fantine</u>, <u>one of his best employees</u>.
(p.32, 8行目)
数年後のある朝、マドレーヌ市長は、とてもよく働くファンティーヌからやっかいな頼みごとをされていた。

【解説】 この文もやはり、先に人名の Fantine を出してから、その働きぶりについて補足しています。ここでも、Fantine と one of his best employees の間にコンマが入っており、はっきり同格であることが示されています。

　本文ではこの前に、She got a job at Mayor Madeleine's factory. （ファンティーヌは、ムッシュ・マドレーヌの工場で働いていた）と、マドレーヌ市長とファンティーヌが示されています。それに続いてこの文で、市長がファンティー

ヌの働きぶりをどう思っていたのかがわかります。

> First, he went to the bank and withdrew six-hundred thousand francs, his entire savings. (p.40, 2行目)
>
> まず、彼は銀行に出かけて60万フランを下ろした。全貯金に相当する額である。

【解説】ここでも具体的に60万フランという金額を出し、その後にコンマで同格であることをはっきり示してから、それが彼（マドレーヌ）の預金のすべてであることを記しています。この物語が書かれた当時、19世紀の60万フランとは、現在の日本円で数億から数十億円に相当します。いずれにしても、マドレーヌがここまでに多額の財産を築いていたことがわかります。

なお、この文がFirstで始まっていることから、次にSecondかNextといった語が続くことを推測できます。「最初に」逮捕される前にまずお金を下ろし、では次には次には何をしたんだろうと、展開を予測ながら読んでいくと、より楽しく物語を味わえます。

> A few years later, another traveler —a young woman—came across an inn in Montfermeil, a suburb of Paris. (p.22, 1行目)
>
> 数年後、若い女性の旅人がパリ郊外のモンフェルメイユにある宿屋にやってきた。

【解説】この文には2つの同格があります。

最初の同格はanother travelerとa young womanで、ここはコンマではなく、ダッシュが使われています。another travelerの前にA few years later, にコンマがあるため、コンマの連続を避けるためにダッシュを用いたものです。同格関係は、このようにダッシュで示されることも多くあります。

なお、この文でanother travelerとあるのは、第1章がa ragged traveler entered a little town. (みすぼらしい身なりの旅人が小さな町にたどり着いた)という文で始まっているのに対して、それとは別の旅人、すなわちファンティーヌがやってきたということを表しています。

2つ目の同格は文の最後、Montfermeilとa suburb of Parisです。ここで初

めて登場するモンフェルメイユという地名を読者に説明するために、後から「パリ郊外」という情報を補足しています。

【例文】ダッシュを使った同格
I was lying on the top of the hill—a sightseeing spot in the town.
私は丘の頂上で横になっていた。この丘は街の観光スポットだった。

Monsieur Madeleine was so popular as an employer and a citizen that <u>everyone in the town</u> gradually came to respect and love him, <u>all except one man</u>. (p.28, 1行目)
ムッシュ・マドレーヌは、雇い主としても市民としても人気が高く、町の人たちはみな、彼のことを敬愛するようになった。しかし一人だけ例外がいた。

【解説】ここでは、everyone in the townとそれを表す同格語句のall except one manの位置が離れています。同格語句はコンマの前の語を指す場合が多いのですが、ここでは、すぐ前のall except one man（一人を除いて）を見れば、単数、複数の違いから、himではないことはすぐにわかります。では誰を指すのかと前をたどってみると、everyoneがあります。「町の全員がムッシュ・マドレーヌを敬愛していた、ただし一人を除いて」と読めば意味がとおることがわかるでしょう。このようにして同格を判断しなければならないこともあります。

　なお、この文にはso〜that構文も使われています。「so+形容詞＋that〜」で、「とても…なので〜である」という意味です。「雇い主としても市民としても人気が高かったので、町の人たちはみな〜するようになった」となります。

48

Part II:
Cosette

コゼット

I

Jean Valjean became Javert's prisoner, but not for long. After his arrest, he was taken to a local jail to await trial. However, that night, Jean Valjean broke out of prison. He went first to his house but left after several minutes. About an hour later, a man was seen walking from Montreuil-sur-Mer toward Paris, carrying a bundle.

A newspaper dated July 25, 1823, reported that an old, wanted convict by the name of Jean Valjean was arrested but had escaped before trial. The convict had gone under the name of Madeleine and become a rich businessman. Before his arrest, he had apparently taken out a large amount of money from his bank account. He was suspected to have hid the money somewhere, but nobody knew where. The man was currently missing.

■break out of prison 脱獄する　■bundle 图包み　■wanted 形指名手配の　■go under the name of 〜の名で通る　■be suspected to 〜した疑いがある

I

　ジャン・ヴァルジャンはジャヴェールに拘束されたが、それも長い間で
はなかった。逮捕後、彼は町の牢屋で裁判を待った。しかしその晩、ジャ
ン・ヴァルジャンは脱獄した。まず自宅へ行ったが、ものの二、三分で出
てきた。一時間ほどたって、モントルイユ＝シュル＝メールからパリに向
けて歩いている男の姿があった。男は包みを一つ携えていた。

　1823年7月25日付の新聞は、長年指名手配されていたジャン・ヴァル
ジャンという名の罪人が逮捕されたが、裁判の前に脱獄したと報じた。罪
人はマドレーヌと名乗り、裕福な実業家となった。逮捕前に、銀行口座か
ら大金を引き出していたようだ。どこかに金を隠したと思われるが、その
在りかを知る者はいない。男は現在行方不明である、と。

コゼット　51

However, a few days later in the town of Montfermeil, an innkeeper by the name of Thénardier was paid a visit by a stranger. The stranger was a gentleman about forty years old. He was a large man with broad shoulders, and his hair was turning white. He came with a doll and a new set of black mourning clothes for a little girl. He carried a bag that held two silver candlesticks and another large bundle. He told Thénardier that he was the legal guardian of Cosette, and that her mother had died. He paid the Thénardiers several thousand francs for looking after the girl, and he left with Cosette. She was seven years old.

■mourning clothes 喪服 ■legal guardian 法定後見人 ■look after ～の世話をする

しかし数日後、モンフェルメイユという町で、テナルディエという名の
宿屋の主を見知らぬ男が訪れた。40歳前後の紳士だった。肩の広い大柄な
男で、髪は白髪がかっていた。紳士は、人形と女の子用の黒い喪服一そろ
いを携えていた。さらに、銀の燭台を二つと、大きな包みを一つ手にしてい
た。紳士はテナルディエに、コゼットの法定後見人であると言い、コゼット
の母親が亡くなったと伝えた。コゼットの世話をしてくれた礼として数千
フランをテナルディエに支払い、紳士はコゼットとともに立ち去った。コ
ゼットは7歳だった。

コゼット　53

II

Beyond the old horse market of Paris, down some very dark and lonely streets, there was a building with only one window facing the street. It was here that Jean Valjean brought Cosette to live. Like a bird of prey, he had chosen this lonely place to make his nest.

For some time, Jean Valjean and Cosette were happy. He adored Cosette, and Cosette loved him dearly, for he was kind, and she had never known kindness with the Thénardiers. She loved to go on walks with Jean Valjean and to play with her doll. Jean Valjean mistakenly thought that they were safe.

Jean Valjean was in the habit of going on a walk every evening. He led a very poor, simple life, but he always gave money to others who needed it more. Despite his hidden identity, he strove every day, every hour, to fulfill his promise to the bishop to be a good man.

■face 動 ~に面する ■bird of prey 猛禽類 ■nest 名巣 ■be in a habit of ~が習慣である ■lead a ~ life ~な生活を送る ■fulfill one's promise 約束を果たす

II

　パリの古い馬市場の先、暗くて人気のない通りを行くと、通りに面する窓がたった一つしかない建物があった。ジャン・ヴァルジャンがコゼットとともに暮らすことにした場所である。鷹のように、ジャン・ヴァルジャンはこの寂しい建物をねぐらにすることに決めたのだ。

　しばらくの間、ジャン・ヴァルジャンとコゼットは幸せに暮らした。ジャン・ヴァルジャンはコゼットをかわいがり、コゼットは彼を心から愛した。やさしかったし、テナルディエ一家の下では、そんなやさしさに触れることはまったくなかったからだ。コゼットはジャン・ヴァルジャンと散歩に出かけたり、人形で遊んだりするのが好きだった。ジャン・ヴァルジャンはもう安全だと思っていたが、それは間違いだった。

　ジャン・ヴァルジャンは毎晩散歩に出かけるのを日課としていた。貧しくつつましい生活を送っていたが、もっと困っている人たちに、いつもお金をめぐんでいた。身元は隠していたが、司教と交わした善人となる約束を果たすために、日々刻々と努力をしてきたのである。

コゼット　55

In Jean Valjean's neighborhood, there was a beggar that sat on the same street every day. Jean Valjean always gave money to this beggar. One day, as Jean Valjean was putting money in his cup as usual, he noticed something strange about the beggar. It was an imposter! Although the man had on the same clothes and sat in the same manner, it was a different man—and he looked like Javert.

That night, Jean Valjean spoke to his landlord and discovered that a new tenant had taken the room next to his. A chill crept up Jean Valjean's spine. He lay awake all night. At one point, he thought he heard someone listening at his door. In that moment, he knew he was no longer safe. He knew that the new tenant must be Javert, who had come to hunt him down.

The next evening, he took Cosette out into the streets on his walk. He tried to hide from her the fact that this was no ordinary walk—they were leaving their home and he was frantically looking for a new place to hide. He knew they had very little time.

■creep up 這い上がる ■lie awake all night 一晩横になって眠れないでいる ■at one point あるとき ■no longer もはや〜でない ■hunt ~ down 〜を追跡して捕える ■no ordinary ただの〜ではない

ジャン・ヴァルジャンの家の近くには乞食がいて、毎日同じ通りに座っていた。ジャン・ヴァルジャンはいつも、その乞食に金をめぐんでいた。ある日、いつもの通りジャン・ヴァルジャンが乞食のお椀に金を入れると、乞食の様子がどこか変なことに気づいた。ペテンだ！　同じ服を着ていつもと同じように座っていたが、別人だった。その男はジャヴェールに似ていた。

　その晩、ジャン・ヴァルジャンは大家と話をした。新しい間借人がジャン・ヴァルジャンの部屋の隣を借りていたことがわかった。ジャン・ヴァルジャンの背筋を冷たいものが走った。一晩中寝つけないでいると、誰かが扉のところで聞き耳を立てているように感じた。その時、彼はもう安全ではないことを悟った。新しい間借人はきっとジャヴェールで、自分を捕まえに来たのだ。

　あくる日の晩、ジャン・ヴァルジャンはコゼットを通りへと散歩に連れだした。いつもの散歩ではなく、家を出て新しい隠れ家を必死に探そうとしていることを、コゼットには隠しておこうとした。もう猶予がないことは分かっていた。

コゼット　57

Suddenly, Jean Valjean heard the sound of a platoon of soldiers behind them. They quickly turned down an alley, but Valjean caught a glimpse of Javert at the head of the platoon, giving orders to search every door and every corner for Jean Valjean.

There was no time! Jean Valjean's eyes darted here and there, looking for some place—any place—to hide. Far down the street, he saw what looked like a walled garden with no gate—it was in a dark, isolated part of the neighborhood, and he could just make out the tops of trees over the tall wall. He would somehow have to get both Cosette and himself into that quiet place. He grabbed Cosette and looked frantically for a way in. Just then, a rope hanging from a light post caught his eye.

With the sound of the soldiers' footsteps and their shouts coming closer, Jean Valjean quickly cut the rope down and tied it around Cosette. He then tied it around his own waist and scaled the wall.

■platoon 名小隊、部隊 ■turn down 脇道に曲がる ■catch a glimpse かいま見る
■give an order to ～するよう命じる ■dart here and there あちこち動き回る
■make out ～を見て取る ■catch one's eye 目に留まる

Part II: Cosette

突然、ジャン・ヴァルジャンは背後から兵士たちがやってくる物音を耳
にした。すぐに通りを曲がっていったが、ジャヴェールが兵士たちの先頭
に立っているのがちらりと見えた。ジャヴェールは、一軒一軒、あらゆる
路地を探すように命じていた。

　もう、一刻を争う事態だ。ジャン・ヴァルジャンの目はめまぐるしく動
き、どこか、どこでもいいので隠れる場所を探した。すると通りのはるか
向こうに、門のない、壁に囲まれた庭のような場所を目にした。この一帯
の中でも暗く、人気のない場所である。高い壁の上に見えるのは木の梢だ
けだ。コゼットと自分の身を、何とかしてあの人目につかない場所に隠さ
なければならない。ジャン・ヴァルジャンはコゼットの腕をつかみ、中に
入る方法を必死に探した。ちょうどその時、街灯からロープが垂れ下がっ
ているのが目に入った。

　兵士たちの足音や叫び声が近づいてくるのを聞きながら、ジャン・ヴァ
ルジャンはロープを急いで切り落とし、コゼットの体に結びつけた。それ
から彼はロープを自分の腰に巻きつけて、壁をよじ登り始めた。

コゼット　59

"Father!" cried Cosette. She was cold, tired, and beginning to realize that something was wrong. She knew they were running from someone.

"Shhh!" replied Jean Valjean when he reached the top of the wall. "Hold on tightly."

He pulled the rope hand over hand, lifting Cosette off the ground and up to the top of the wall. Putting her on his back, he carefully crawled down the wall and dropped into the dark garden. When he landed, a man's voice cried, "Stop! Who are you?"

■run from ～から逃げる　■hold on しっかりつかまる　■hand over hand（ロープなどを）両手でたぐって　■lift ~ off ～を…から持ち上げる　■up to the top てっぺんまで　■put ~ on one's back ～を背負う　■land 働 着地する

「お父さん！」とコゼットは叫んだ。疲れて凍えていたし、何か変だと気づき始めていた。誰かから逃げていることに気がついたのである。

ジャン・ヴァルジャンは、壁のてっぺんに到達すると「シー！」と答えた。「しっかりつかまっていなさい」

彼はロープを両手でたぐってコゼットを地面から引き上げ、壁のてっぺんまで持ち上げた。コゼットを背負い、壁を慎重につたい降りて、暗い庭へと降り立った。地面につくと、男が声を張り上げた。「おい！　お前は誰だ」

III

*J*ean Valjean slowly turned around, holding Cosette. If they weren't allowed to hide in this garden, Javert would certainly catch them. What would happen to Cosette then? He shuddered at the thought.

Desperate, Jean Valjean said, "I'm very sorry, sir, but my daughter and I need to stay here for the night. Please, have pity on us. Please, let us stay."

In the darkness, it was hard to see the man, who was holding up a lantern and studying them.

"My God!" said the man. "Mayor Madeleine! What are you doing here? It's me, don't you remember? Fauchelevent! You saved my life years ago in Montreuil-sur-Mer. You lifted a cart off me!"

A great wave of relief washed over Jean Valjean, and he embraced the man he had once saved.

■turn around 振り向く ■shudder at 〜を恐れて身震いする ■have pity on 〜を哀れむ ■hold up 持ち上げる ■study 動 〜を観察する ■wash over 〜にどっと押し寄せる

III

　ジャン・ヴァルジャンは、コゼットを腕に抱いたまま、ゆっくり振り返った。この庭に隠れることができなければ、きっとジャヴェールに捕まってしまう。そうしたら、コゼットはどうなるのだ。こう考えると身震いがした。

　ジャン・ヴァルジャンは必死に訴えた。「申し訳ありません。でも、娘と私は今晩ここにいなければならないのです。どうぞお慈悲を。私たちをここにいさせて下さい」

　暗闇の中で、声の主を見分けることは難しかった。その男は、ランタンを掲げて二人の様子を見ていた。

　「なんと！」と男は言った。「マドレーヌ市長ではありませんか！　ここで何をなさっているのですか。私です。お忘れですか、ずっと前にモントルイユ＝シュル＝メールで私の命を救っていただいた、フォーシュルヴァンです！　私の上に倒れた荷車をどかしてくれたのです！」

　ジャン・ヴァルジャンは大きな安堵に包まれて、かつて命を救った男を抱きしめた。

コゼット　63

"Fauchelevent!" he said. "It's good to see you. We have some trouble. I cannot tell you about it, but my daughter is cold and needs a bed. Will you let us stay?"

"You can hide here in the garden for the night, but you can't stay any longer. This is a convent! Only the nuns are allowed to stay here. I'm allowed to stay only because I am their gardener."

Carrying Cosette, Jean Valjean gratefully followed Fauchelevent to a shack where a small bed was set up. After Cosette was asleep, the two men talked.

"We must stay here," said Jean Valjean. "We cannot go back to the city; it is too dangerous for us. I cannot explain why, but remember that I saved your life. You can save ours now by letting us stay."

"I know I owe you my life, and I'd like to help. But it's not up to me. To stay, you have to get permission from the Mother Superior."

"Perhaps you can help me get permission."

■any longer これ以上　■convent 图修道院　■shack 图小屋　■owe ~ one's life ～は命の恩人である　■up to ～次第で　■Mother Superior 女子修道院長

64　Part II: Cosette

「フォーシュルヴァン！」とジャン・ヴァルジャンは言った。「お会いできてよかった。厄介なことに巻き込まれまして。詳しいことは言えないのですが、娘が凍えてしまって、ベッドが必要なのです。どうか泊めていただけないでしょうか」

「夜の間は庭に潜んでいてもかまいません。でも、その後は居るわけにはいきません。ここは修道院なのです！　ここにいてよいのは修道女だけです。私は庭師だから許されているのですが」

感謝しつつ、ジャン・ヴァルジャンはコゼットを連れてフォーシュルヴァンの後を歩き、小屋についた。小さなベッドが準備されていた。コゼットが眠りについたあと、二人の男は話をした。

「私たちはここにいなければなりません」とジャン・ヴァルジャンは言った。「町に戻ることはできません。危険すぎます。訳は言えませんが、私があなたの命の恩人であることを思い出してください。私たちをここにいさせてくれれば、今度は私たちの命が助けられる番です」

「ええ、あなたは私の命の恩人ですし、お力になりたいと思います。でも、私の一存で決まるわけではありません。ここに留まるには、修道院長の許可が必要です」

「許可を取る手助けをしていただけないでしょうか」

コゼット　65

Fauchelevent did not get much sleep that night. He was thinking about his old mayor's request. But the next day, with his mind made up, Fauchelevent introduced the former mayor as his brother, Ultimus Fauchelevent, and Cosette as his brother's daughter. After a long conversation, the Mother Superior enrolled Cosette at the convent school and Ultimus Fauchelevent was allowed to stay as an assistant gardener at the convent. They were saved.

Jean Valjean and Cosette found happiness again. Cosette was good at her studies, and she was allowed to visit Jean Valjean every day for an hour. They lived a quiet, content life as the years passed and Cosette grew up.

■with one's mind made up 決心して　■as the years pass 年月がすぎるにつれて
■grow up 成長する

フォーシュルヴァンは、その晩あまり眠れなかった。かつての市長の頼みについて考えていたからだ。しかし翌日、心を決めたフォーシュルヴァンは、元市長を弟のユルティム・フォーシュルヴァン、コゼットを弟の娘だと紹介した。長い間話し合って、修道院長はコゼットを修道院の付属学校に入学させ、ユルティム・フォーシュルヴァンは庭師助手として修道院に留まることが許された。二人は救われたのである。

　ジャン・ヴァルジャンとコゼットは、幸せを取り戻した。コゼットは勉強がよくでき、毎日一時間ジャン・ヴァルジャンの下を訪れることを許された。歳月が経ってコゼットが成長する中、二人は静かで満ち足りた生活を送った。

確かな読解のための英語表現 ［文法］

関係代名詞 **who**と**that**

名詞の後ろに置かれて、説明を加えるときに使われる表現のひとつが関係代名詞です。関係代名詞によって修飾される名詞を先行詞と呼び、この先行詞が人の場合に用いられる関係代名詞がwho（またはthat）です。

He led a very poor, simple life, but he always gave money to others <u>who</u> needed it more. （p.54, 下から4行目）

ジャン・ヴァルジャンは貧しくつつましい生活を送っていたが、もっと困っている人たちに、いつもお金をめぐんでいた。

【解説】関係代名詞whoがothersを後ろから修飾しています。others who needed it more（それをもっと必要としている他の人々）という意味になります。このように、関係代名詞が後ろから先行詞を修飾する用法を、限定用法といいます。ここでは先行詞othersについて、「（他の人々の中でも）もっとそれを必要としている人」に限定しています。なお、このitが指すものは、その前にある名詞をたどっていくとmoneyということがわかります。

He knew that the new tenant must be Javert, who had come to hunt him down. （p.56, 下から8行目）

新しい間借人はきっとジャヴェールで、自分を捕まえに来たのだと悟った。

【解説】このwhoは、関係代名詞の前にコンマがあります。こういう使い方を関係代名詞の継続用法といい、who had come to hunt him downはJavertを修飾するのではなく、Javertに説明をくわえる役目をしています。このコンマを取ってしまうと限定用法となり、「彼を捕まえに来たジャヴェール」という意味、すなわち何人かいるうちのジャヴェールのひとりが、彼を捕まえに来たという意味になってしまいます。

In the darkness, it was hard to see the man, <u>who</u> was holding up a lantern and studying them. (p.62, 8行目)

暗闇の中で、声の主を見分けることは難しかった。その男は、ランタンを掲げて二人の様子を見ていた。

【解説】これも、whoの前にコンマがあるので、関係代名詞の継続用法です。who was holding up a lantern and studying themは、the manを説明する情報です。

In Jean Valjean's neighborhood, there was a beggar <u>that</u> sat on the same street every day. (p.56, 1行目)

ジャン・ヴァルジャンの家の近くには乞食がいて、毎日同じ通りに座っていた。

【解説】ここではwhoではなくthatが使われていますが、これも前のa beggarを後ろから修飾する、限定用法の関係代名詞です。「毎日同じ通りに座っているひとりの乞食がいた」という意味になります。

分詞構文

動詞の原形＋ing（現在分詞）、動詞の原形＋ed（過去分詞）で作る分詞句が副詞として働き、文（主節）を修飾する用法を分詞構文と言います。分詞構文は、意味として、時、理由、状況説明（〜しながら）を表すことが大半と言えます。

About an hour later, a man was seen walking from Montreuil-sur-Mer toward Paris, <u>carrying</u> a bundle. (p.50, 4行目)

一時間ほどたって、モントルイユ＝シュル＝メールからパリに向けて歩いている男の姿があった。男は包みを一つ携えていた。

【解説】ここで、carrying a bundle（包みを携えている）が、a man was seen walking from Montreuil-sur-Mer toward Paris（モントルイユ＝シュル＝メールからパリに向けて歩いている男）を修飾し、「〜しながら」という状況を説明する働きをしています。

69

Jean Valjean's eyes darted here and there, <u>looking</u> for some place—any place—to hide. (p.58, 6行目)

ジャン・ヴァルジャンの目はめまぐるしく動き、どこか、どこでもいいので隠れる場所を探した。

【解説】ここではlookingの分詞句は、目がdart（素早く動く）するという動作、そしてlook for some place（どこかの場所を求める）という動作を続けて行ったことを表しています。接続詞andを用いて、Jean Valjean's eyes darted here and there and looked for some place—any place—to hide. と言い換えることもできます。

　なお、ここでダッシュに挟まれているany placeとその前のsome placeは、46〜48ページで解説した同格関係にあります。some place（どこか）と記してから、any place（どこでも）と言い換えているのです。

He pulled the rope hand over hand, <u>lifting</u> Cosette off the ground and up to the top of the wall. (p.60, 6行目)

彼はロープを両手でたぐってコゼットを地面から引き上げ、壁のてっぺんまで持ち上げた。

【解説】これも動作の連続を表します。andを用いてHe pulled the rope hand over hand and lifted Cosette off the groundとすることもできるのですが、この後にand up toがあるため、liftの前にandを使用せずに分詞構文にしたと考えられます。

<u>Carrying</u> Cosette, Jean Valjean gratefully followed Fauchelevent to a shack where a small bed was set up. (p.64, 8行目)

感謝しつつ、ジャン・ヴァルジャンはコゼットを連れてフォーシュルヴァンの後を歩き、小屋についた。小さなベッドが準備されていた。

【解説】この分詞構文も状況説明です。「コゼットを連れたまま、フォーシュルヴァンの後をついていった」という意味を表します。

Part III: Marius

マリウス

I

$\mathcal{M}$arius had lived with his grandfather, Monsieur Gillenormand, and his aunt, Mademoiselle Gillenormand, for as long as he could remember. He had no idea that his father had been a colonel under Napoleon Bonaparte, nor that his father had been given the title of baron for his bravery at war. Indeed, Baron Pontmercy was a war hero whose courage was unrivalled. However, after Napoleon was exiled, the restoration took away his title and pension, and Baron Pontmercy was forced to live as a poor man.

■have no idea that ～なんて全く知らない　■nor 腰 ～もまた…ない　■title of bron 男爵の称号　■exile 動 国外追放する　■take away ～を剥奪する　■pension 图恩給　■be forced to ～せざるを得ない

I

　マリウスは物心ついてからというもの、祖父のムッシュ・ジルノルマン、叔母のマダモアゼル・ジルノルマンとともに暮らしていた。父がナポレオン・ボナパルトの大佐であり、武勲で男爵の地位を与えられていたことなど、知る由もなかった。実際、ポンメルシー男爵は戦争の英雄で、勇猛さにおいて右に出る者はいなかった。しかし、ナポレオンが島流しになり王政復古の時代になると、ポンメルシーは爵位も恩給も剥奪され、貧困のうちに生きることを強いられた。

マリウス　73

Marius's mother, who was the daughter of Monsieur Gillenormand, died when Marius was still a baby. After her death, Monsieur Gillenormand decided that he would raise Marius. Monsieur Gillenormand was a wealthy, old bourgeois and royalist. He had plenty of money and important connections to help Marius in life. Monsieur Gillenormand threatened to cut off Marius's significant inheritance if Pontmercy did not give up the boy.

Baron Pontmercy, who loved his son very much, allowed him to be adopted by his grandfather. He knew he could not give Marius the life that Monsieur Gillenormand could. Monsieur Gillenormand, on the other hand, firmly believed that Baron Pontmercy was a traitor and a fool, and more importantly a bad influence on the young boy. He did not ever let Marius see his father.

The first and only time Marius saw his father was when he was eighteen years old. He came home from law school one evening to see his grandfather reading a letter.

"You will travel to Vernon tomorrow," his grandfather said, looking up from the letter. "Your father is sick."

■bourgeois 图 ブルジョワ、有産階級　■cut off 〜を絶つ　■inheritance 图 遺産　■give up 〜を放棄する　■traitor 图 反逆者　■let 〜 see 〜を…に会わせる

マリウスの母親はムッシュ・ジルノルマンの娘であったが、マリウスが
赤ん坊の頃に亡くなった。娘の死後、ジルノルマンは自らマリウスを育て
ることにした。ムッシュ・ジルノルマンは裕福で昔ながらのブルジョワで、
王政主義者だった。大いに資産があり、マリウスの人生を支えてくれる要
人の人脈もあった。ムッシュ・ジルノルマンは、ポンメルシーが孫の親権
をあきらめなければマリウスの相続分を大幅に減らすと脅したのである。

ポンメルシー男爵は息子を心から愛していたが、祖父と息子との養子縁
組を認めた。ムッシュ・ジルノルマンがもたらせる生活を、自分は息子に
与えてやれないことが分かっていたからだ。一方ムッシュ・ジルノルマン
は、ポンメルシー男爵が愚鈍な裏切り者であり、さらに重大なことに、マ
リウスに悪い影響を与えていると頑なに信じていた。だから、マリウスを
父親に決して会わせなかったのである。

マリウスが初めて、そしてただ一度父親に会いまみえたのは、18歳の時
だった。ある日、法律学校から帰ってきたマリウスは、祖父が手紙を読ん
でいるのに気づいた。
「明日ヴァーノンに行きなさい」と祖父は手紙から目を上げて言った。「お
前の父が病気なのだ」

Marius did as he was told, but when he arrived at his father's house, he realized he was too late. His father lay in his bed, his eyes closed and his hands crossed over his chest. The priest was there, keeping vigil. Baron Pontmercy was dead.

Marius, having never known this dead man, felt very little. The priest handed him a piece of paper, which had a few lines written on it.

"This is for you," said the priest. "Your father talked only of you until the very end."

Marius opened the note. It read, "For my son—The emperor made me a baron upon the battlefield of Waterloo. Since the restoration contests this title which I have bought with my blood, my son will take it and bear it. I need not say that he will be worthy of it."

Marius went back home to Monsieur Gillenormand. He wore some black crepe on his hat for his father. That was all.

■keep vigil 通夜をする　■until the very end 最後の最後まで　■read 動(文字が)書いてある　■buy with one's blood 命をかけて手に入れる　■worthy of 〜にふさわしい

マリウスは言われたとおりにしたが、父の家に着いた時には、もう手遅れだとわかった。ベッドに横たわった父は目を閉じて、両手を胸の上で組んでいた。司教が通夜を営んでいた。ポンメルシー男爵はこの世を去ったのだ。

マリウスは、この亡くなった男を知らなかったので、たいして心が動かされることもなかった。司教はマリウスに紙切れを渡した。そこには数行の文字が記されていた。

「これはあなたへの手紙です」と司教は言った。「お父様は、最期まであなたのことばかりお話ししていましたよ」

マリウスは紙を開いた。そこにはこう書いてあった。「息子よ。ウォータールーの戦いのあと、ナポレオン皇帝は私を男爵とした。私が命を賭けて勝ち取ったこの爵位は王政復古により失われたが、息子が引き継いで名乗るものとする。お前がこの称号に値することは言うまでもなかろう」

マリウスはムッシュ・ジルノルマンの住む家へと帰った。父を悼み、帽子の上に黒いちりめんの布を被せていたが、それだけのことであった。

マリウス　77

II

Marius always went to church on Sunday, and he preferred to go to the church where his aunt had brought him every week as a child. One Sunday a few months after his father's death, Marius went to this church. Being in a rather dreamy mood, he decided to kneel down behind a particular pillar to pray.

Suddenly, a man approached him and said, "My dear sir, you are praying in a special spot."

"What do you mean?" asked Marius.

"Will you allow me to tell you the story? You see, a man who was separated from his son used to come here every Sunday and hide behind this pillar to see his son. He had no other way of seeing him, because the boy had been adopted by his grandfather. The grandfather threatened to disinherit the boy if the father did not give him up, so, the father sacrificed his own happiness so that the boy could have a good life. When he saw his son here every week, he would weep.

■as a child 子供のころに　■kneel down ひざまずく　■my dear sir あなたさま
■used to 以前は〜したものだった　■have no other way of 他に〜の手だてがない
■so that 〜できるように

78　Part III: Marius

II

　マリウスは日曜に決まって教会に行ったが、なかでも、子供のころ伯母が毎週連れていってくれた教会に行くのを好んだ。父の死から数か月経ったある日曜日のこと、マリウスはこの教会に出かけた。どこか夢見心地で、ある柱の裏手にひざまずいて祈りを捧げることにした。

　突然、ある男が近づいてきてこう言った。「あなたは特別な場所で祈りを捧げているのですよ」

　「どういうことですか」とマリウスはたずねた。

　「お話ししてもよろしいですか。息子から引き離された男が毎週日曜日にこの教会に来て、この柱の陰に潜んで息子の様子を伺っていたのです。息子は祖父の養子にされて、息子と会う術はほかにありませんでした。祖父はその父親に、息子を手放さなければ息子に遺産を継がせないと脅したので、父親は自分の幸せを犠牲にして、息子がよい生活を送れるようにしたのです。父親は毎週この場所から息子を見て泣いていました。

He loved the boy very much. It was very tragic because the father and son were separated for political reasons—the father had been a colonel for Napoleon, and he had fought bravely at Waterloo. That does not make a man a monster! But the grandfather thought the man was a traitor and would not let him near the boy. The man's name was something like Pontmarie or Montpercy. He had a handsome scar on his face from battle."

"Pontmercy," said Marius, turning pale.

"What? Oh, yes! Pontmercy. Did you know him?"

"He was my father."

The man gave an exclamation of surprise.

Marius offered his arm to the man and walked him home, asking him all about his father.

The next day, Marius said to his grandfather, "I'd like to go on a hunting trip with some friends. May I go away for three days?"

"Four," said his grandfather. "Go. Have fun."

■make ~ a monster ～を怪物に変える　■handsome 彫堂々たる　■give an exclamation of surprise 驚きの声をあげる　■offer one's arm to ～に腕を差し出す
■go on a trip 旅行する

息子のことをとても愛していたのです。政治的なことで父親と息子が引き
離されたのは、不幸な悲劇というほかありません。父親はナポレオン軍の
大佐で、ウォータールーでは勇敢に戦いました。そんなことで人が怪物に
なるわけもありません。でも、祖父はその男のことを裏切り者と決めつけ
て、息子の傍に近づけなかったのです。父親は、ポンマリとか、モンペル
シとかいう名前でした。戦いでつけられた大きな傷が顔にありましたよ」

　「ポンメルシーではないですか」とマリウスは言った。顔から血の気が引
いていた。
　「なんですって。そうです！　ポンメルシーです。ご存じですか」
　「ポンメルシーは私の父でした」
　男は、驚きのあまり叫び声をあげた。
　マリウスは男に腕を差し出し、歩いて彼の家へと向かう途中で、父のこ
とをあれこれとたずねた。
　翌日、マリウスは祖父に言った。「友人と狩りに出かけたいのです。三日
間留守にしてもいいですか」
　「四日でもかまわない」と祖父は答えた。「行って楽しんでおいで」

III

Marius was gone for three days, but he wasn't hunting with friends. He went straight to the library of his law school, where he read every newspaper, book, and record he could that mentioned his father or the battle of Waterloo. His father had been a good, noble, brave man. Marius was starting to love the father he never knew. He was also starting to understand his father's politics. All his life, he had taken his grandfather's beliefs as his own opinions. Now he was starting to see things in a different way—to learn a new philosophy.

Marius was gone from home quite often, pursuing this new passion. He also developed a habit of taking flowers to his father's grave.

Back at home, Mademoiselle Gillenormand would wonder out loud to Monsieur Gillenormand, "Where does that boy go all the time?"

■go straight to 〜に直行する ■take a belief as one's own （ある）信念を自分の信念として受け入れる ■philosophy 图哲学 ■develop a habit of 〜の習慣を身に付ける ■wonder out loud 声高にたずねる

III

　マリウスは三日間出かけていたが、友人と狩りをしていたわけではなかった。法律学校の図書館へとまっすぐ向かい、父やウォータールーの戦いについて触れた新聞や本、記録を片っ端から読んだのである。父は善良で気高く、勇敢な男だった。マリウスは、直には知らない父のことを愛し始めていた。また、父の政治的立場についても理解するようになった。生まれてこのかた、マリウスは祖父の信念を自分の考えとして受け入れていたのだ。しかし今や、マリウスは別の視点から物事をとらえようとしていた。新たな哲学を学びつつあったのである。

　こうした新たな情熱に突き動かされて、マリウスは家を空けることが増えた。また、父の墓に花を供えるのを慣わしとするようになった。

　家に戻ると、マダモアゼル・ジルノルマンはムッシュ・ジルノルマンに向かって、「この子はいつもどこにいくのかしら」と声高にたずねた。

マリウス　83

Monsieur Gillenormand believed Marius was seeing some girl or another. But Marius was reading, and book by book, Marius shed his old bourgeois skin and his royalism. He gained a passion for the republic, and when he finally became fully revolutionary, he went to a card-maker in town and ordered a hundred name cards that read, "Baron Marius Pontmercy."

Meanwhile, his aunt and grandfather became more and more curious about Marius's mysterious trips.

One day, when Marius returned from one of his trips, his grandfather followed him to his room. Marius took off his coat and the little box he had started to wear around his neck. He laid these on his bed, and he went into the bathroom to take a bath.

■book by book 本を読むごとに　■shed one's skin 脱皮する　■meanwhile 副その間に　■become curious about ～が気になる　■take a bath 入浴する

84　Part III: Marius

ムッシュ・ジルノルマンは、マリウスがどこかの女とあい引きしている
のだろうと思っていた。しかし、マリウスは本を読んでいた。そして、読
み進めるごとに、これまでのブルジョワジーや王政主義の考えから脱皮し
ていった。共和主義への情熱を育み、ついに革命の魂を宿すと、町の名刺
屋に出向いて名刺を100枚注文した。「マリウス・ポンメルシー男爵」と書
かれた名刺だ。

　その間、伯母と祖父は、マリウスの不可解な旅行について不信を募らせ
ていた。
　ある日、マリウスが旅行から戻ってくると、祖父はマリウスの自室につ
いて行った。マリウスは外套を脱ぎ、近頃かけるようになった小さい箱を
首から外した。マリウスはこれらの品をベッドの上に置き、入浴しに浴室
へと向かった。

マリウス　85

His grandfather, stepping into his room, found the box and opened it. There, folded carefully, he found a piece of paper with a few lines written on it. It was Baron Pontmercy's letter to his son, giving him the title of baron. This quite shocked Monsieur Gillenormand, and he continued to search Marius's things. What he found next almost stopped his heart: in Marius's coat pocket, wrapped in blue paper, were one hundred name cards that read "Baron Marius Pontmercy."

When Marius came out of his bath, he found himself facing his grandfather, who was shaking with fury. The two men—one young, one old—fought passionately. Finally, Monsieur Gillenormand said quietly, "A baron like Monsieur and a bourgeois like myself cannot stay under the same roof."

The next day, Marius left his grandfather's house.

■step into ～に立ち入る　■line 図（文章の）行　■find oneself doing ～する羽目になる　■shake with fury 怒りに震える　■under the same roof 同じ屋根の下で

86　Part III: Marius

祖父はマリウスの部屋に入り、箱を見つけて開けてみた。そこには、ていねいに畳まれた紙片があった。数行の文字が記されている。ポンメルシー男爵が息子に宛てた手紙で、マリウスに男爵の称号を与えるものであった。ムッシュ・ジルノルマンは強い衝撃を受けて、マリウスの私物を探し続けた。次に見つけたものは、ムッシュ・ジルノルマンの心臓を止めそうになった。マリウスの外套のポケットには青い紙に包まれた100枚の名刺があり、「マリウス・ポンメルシー男爵」と書かれていたのだ。

　マリウスは浴室から出てきて、祖父と向き合った。祖父は怒りで震えていた。二人の男たちは、かたや若く、かたや老いていたが、激しく言い争った。ついに、ムッシュ・ジルノルマンは静かに言った。「あなたのような男爵と、私のようなブルジョワが一つ屋根の下に住むわけにはいきませんな」

　次の日、マリウスは祖父の家を後にした。

IV

*L*ife became stern to Marius. Marius continued to go to school, but without his grandfather's financial support, he was very poor. He lived in a shabby, broken-down apartment and he was hungry most of the time. However, he was very inventive and resourceful. He found ways to make a small loaf of bread last for three meals. Somehow he got through law school, and upon graduation he found work. When Marius discovered that he was able to support himself, he felt a surge of pride. He was still poor, but he was happy that he had taught himself how to survive. He had made his own life for himself.

By the time Marius was twenty years old, he lived comfortably in a small apartment, and he worked hard to provide for himself. He had two suits: a new one for special occasions, and an old one, which was for every day. He liked to go for a walk in the Luxembourg every afternoon.

■broken-down 形ボロボロの　■find a way to 〜する方法を見つける　■get through 〜をやり終える　■last for 〜のあいだ持続する　■teach oneself how to 〜の方法を独学する

IV

マリウスはつらい人生を歩み始めた。学校に行き続けたが、祖父の経済的な支援がなくなり、とても貧しくなった。崩れかけのみすぼらしいアパルトマンに住み、だいたいいつも腹を空かせていた。しかし、マリウスは工夫や機転で乗り切った。小さなパンのかたまりで三食分持たせる方法を思いついたりしたのだ。何とか法律学校の課程を終え、卒業すると職を得た。自活できることがわかり、マリウスは大きな誇りを感じた。まだ貧しかったが、生き延びる術を身につけられたことがうれしかった。自力で自分の人生をつかみ取ったのである。

20歳になるころ、マリウスは小さなアパルトマンで楽しく暮らし、生計を立てるために必死に働いた。マリウスは服を二着持っていた。特別な機会のために新調した服と、日常使い用の古い服である。毎日午後になるとリュクサンブール公園を散歩した。

マリウス　89

Marius had become very handsome, and young women turned to look at him when he walked by. But he always assumed they were looking at his old suit and laughing at his frayed collar and sleeves. This made Marius very nervous of women in general. There were only two women in the world that didn't make him nervous. They were his old landlady, and a young girl he barely even noticed.

This young girl walked in the Luxembourg every day with a man whom Marius assumed was her father. The girl wore the shabby, black clothes of a convent school uniform. She seemed about thirteen or fourteen years old, and she was so skinny and pale that she was almost ugly. Her father was a large, powerful-looking man with white hair. Privately, Marius called the girl Mademoiselle Black for her dress and the man Monsieur White for his hair.

At a certain point one year, Marius became very busy with his work and he did not go to the park for many months. Then, finally, he found some free time and was able to stroll along the Luxembourg's avenue of trees again. There he saw Monsieur White walking with a beautiful woman. She wore an elegant black dress and a white hat. She was so striking that Marius got quite confused and nervous.

■turn to look at 振り返って～を見る　■walk by 通りかかる　■in general 総じて
■barely even ～すらほとんどしない　■at a certain point ある時点で　■stroll
along ～沿いをぶらつく

90　Part III: Marius

マリウスはとても凛々しくなり、近くを通りかかると若い女性たちが振り返った。でもマリウスは、女性たちは古い服を見て、縁のすり切れた襟や袖のことを笑っているのだろうといつも思っていた。こうしてマリウスは、女性全般に対して神経過敏になった。マリウスが神経を尖らせないで済む女性は、この世に二人しかいなかった。老いた女家主と、たいして気にも留めていなかった少女だけである。

　この少女は、リュクサンブール公園を毎日散歩していた。男性が一緒で、たぶん父親だろうとマリウスは思っていた。少女は質素な黒い服を着ていた。修道学校の制服である。13歳か14歳に見えた。やせこけて青白く、醜いといってもいいぐらいだった。父親は大柄で力の強そうな男性で、髪は白かった。心の中で、マリウスは少女をマダモアゼル・ブラック、男性をムッシュ・ホワイトと呼んでいた。もちろん、少女の服と男性の髪から取った名前である。

　ある年のあるとき、マリウスは仕事がとても忙しく、何か月も公園に行けないでいた。その後ついに少し時間に余裕ができて、リュクサンブール公園の並木通りを歩けるようになった。マリウスはそこで、ムッシュ・ホワイトが美しい女性と歩いているのを目にした。女性は優美な黒い服と白い帽子を身に着けていた。あまりに目を引いたので、マリウスはまごついて神経が高ぶった。

When he stole another look at the young woman, he almost fell over—it was Mademoiselle Black! She was all grown up and so womanly. She must have now been fifteen or so.

"What a difference a summer can make in a young girl's life!" thought Marius. As he stared, almost dumbfounded, at her, the girl looked back at him. She smiled. Marius dropped his eyes and began to sweat. He turned around and quickly walked the other way without quite knowing where he was going.

"She smiled! She smiled!" he thought. Then he looked down at the old suit he was wearing and his heart sank.

"She must be laughing at this shabby suit!" he thought.

The next day, Marius put on his new suit and went to the park. He walked past Mademoiselle Black and Monsieur White. He pretended not to notice them. Then he sat on a bench and pretended to read a newspaper, but really he was staring over the top of it at Mademoiselle Black. In this way, Marius saw the young woman every day, and each day made him fall more in love with her.

■steal a look at 〜を盗み見る　■fall over 倒れる　■drop one's eyes 視線を落とす
■stare over 〜 at …を〜越しに見つめる　■fall in love with 〜に恋する

92　Part III: Marius

若い女性をもう一度見ると、地面に倒れこみそうになった。マダモアゼル・ブラックだ！　大人になり、とても女らしくなっていた。もう15歳ぐらいだろう。

　「ひと夏で、若い女性の人生はこんなに変わるものか」とマリウスは考えた。驚きのあまり声もでなくなったマリウスがただ見つめていると、少女も見つめ返してきた。少女はほほえんだ。マリウスは視線を落として、汗をかき始めた。振り返って反対方向へと足早に歩きだしたが、どこへ行こうとしているのか、自分でもわからなかった。

　「あの娘はほほえんだ！　あの娘はほほえんだ！」と彼は考えた。それから、身に着けている古い服を見て、心が沈んだ。

　「きっと、このぼろぼろの服のことを笑ってるのだろう」と彼は思った。

　あくる日、マリウスは新しい服を着て公園に向かった。彼はマダモアゼル・ブラックとムッシュ・ホワイトの横を通り過ぎたが、気づかないふりをした。それからベンチに腰掛けて新聞を読んでいるふりをしたが、実際には新聞の上からマダモアゼル・ブラックを見つめていた。こうして、マリウスはマダモアゼル・ブラックを毎日眺めては、日に日に恋に落ちていった。

V

Meanwhile, Marius was oblivious to the other people in his world, such as the family of four who lived in the room next to his. Their name was Thénardier, and they were very poor—in fact, they were quite miserable.

Several months before, Marius had overheard the landlady saying she was going to evict the family because they had not paid rent in six months. In a moment of compassion, Marius had given her all the money he had to pay their rent. He asked her not to tell the neighbors it was from him, but somehow they found out. In the meantime, busy with his work and the discovery of Mademoiselle Black's transformation, Marius forgot all about them.

One day, Marius heard a knock at his door. It was Eponine, the elder daughter of the Thénardier family. Although she was a pretty girl, she was dirty and thin, and her shirt was ripped.

■oblivious to ～に気づかない　■evict 動 立ち退かせる　■pay rent 家賃を支払う
■in a moment すぐに、一瞬にして　■find out 突き止める

94　Part III: Marius

V

　その間、マリウスは近くにいる他の人々、彼の住む部屋の隣に住む四人家族の動静にも全く気づかなかった。彼らはテナルディエという名前で、とても貧しかった。実のところ、とてもみじめな様子だった。

　数か月前、テナルディエ一家は家賃を半年も払っていないので、追い出すつもりだと女家主が言っているのをマリウスは漏れ聞いた。憐みの心が芽生えたマリウスは、ありったけのお金を女家主に渡して、一家の家賃に充ててもらった。この金は自分が払ったということを隣人には言わないようにと頼んでおいたが、どういうわけか、テナルディエ一家は金の出所を突き止めた。その間、仕事も忙しかったしマダモアゼル・ブラックの変容ぶりに気も取られていたので、マリウスはそのことをすっかり忘れていた。

　ある日、自室の扉をノックする音をマリウスは耳にした。テナルディエ一家の長女エポニーヌだった。かわいらしい少女だったが、薄汚れて痩せており、シャツは破れていた。

マリウス　95

"Monsieur Marius!" she said with a smile. "I have a letter for you."

And she stepped into his room without an invitation.

Marius opened the letter and read it while Eponine went around his room and looked at his things. The letter was from Eponine's father, Monsieur Thénardier. He thanked Marius for being so generous to his family in the past. Eventually, Marius got to the point of the letter—Thénardier was asking for more money.

Marius gave Eponine five francs. Watching the poor girl made Marius realize that although he was poor, he had never known real misery as this girl had. Eponine went away, and Marius spent the rest of the day thinking about how so many people in the world were as miserable as the Thénardiers. He had heard that the family had once owned an inn in a suburb of Paris, but the inn had failed and the family had no other income.

How cruel life could be, thought Marius.

Pondering these things, Marius noticed a hole in the upper corner of his wall. It looked down into the Thénardiers' room. Unable to control his curiosity, he decided to look into their apartment to see what their lives were like.

■without an invitation 招待なしに　■go around 歩き回る　■get to the point 核心に触れる　■make ~ realize ~に気づかせる　■ponder 動 思案する

96　Part III: Marius

「ムッシュ・マリウス」とエポニーヌはほほえんで言った。「あなた宛ての手紙です」

そして、エポニーヌは招かれもしないのに部屋に入ってきた。

マリウスが手紙を開けて読んでいると、エポニーヌは部屋を見回して、マリウスの私物を見ていた。手紙は、エポニーヌの父親、ムッシュ・テナルディエからだった。ムッシュ・テナルディエは、一家に対して前にとても親切にしてくれたことを感謝していた。読み進めるうちに、何が言いたいのかぴんときた。テナルディエはまた、金を無心しているのだ。

マリウスはエポニーヌに5フラン渡した。気の毒な少女を見ているうちに、自分も貧しいけれどもこの子が味わっているような本当のみじめさは知らないな、と気づいた。エポニーヌは出ていき、マリウスはその日の残りを、世の中にはテナルディエ一家のようにみじめな暮らしをする人たちがどれほどいるのだろうと思いながら過ごした。テナルディエ一家はかつてパリ郊外で宿を営んでいたが、経営に失敗し、ほかに収入を得る術もなかったのだ。

人生とは残酷だなと、マリウスは考えた。

こんな考えを巡らせているうち、マリウスは、壁の上隅に穴が開いているのに気がついた。穴はテナルディエ一家の部屋を見下ろしている。好奇心に勝てず、マリウスは一家のアパルトマンをのぞき込み、暮らしぶりを見てやろうとした。

VI

As Marius watched, Eponine entered the room. She must have spent some time out in town.

"He is coming! The gentleman is coming!" she cried.

The father stood up.

"How do you know? How did you do it?" he asked.

"I went to church, just like you asked, and I handed him your letter. He read it, then he asked for my address. I told him to follow me, but he said he would go shopping before he came. I came home and waited outside, and I just saw his carriage coming down the street!"

"Good! We must prepare!" said the father.

To Marius's shock, the father threw some water on the fire to put it out, then he kicked the seat off of the only chair in the house. He told his wife to get into bed and act sick. Then he told his younger daughter to break the glass in the window.

■just like 〜の通りに ■ask for someone's address (人の) 住所を尋ねる ■come down a street 通りをやってくる ■put out (火を) 消す ■kick 〜 off 〜を蹴り飛ばす ■get into bed ベッドに入る

VI

　マリウスが見ていると、エポニーヌが部屋に入ってきた。しばらく町に
いたのだろう。
　「あの方が来る！　あの方がいらっしゃるわ！」とエポニーヌは叫んだ。
　父は立ち上がった。
　「どうしてわかる。どうやって知った」と父は聞いた。
　「お父さんが言ったように、教会へ行って、あの方に手紙を渡したの。あ
の方は手紙を読んで、私の住所を聞いてきた。ついて来てって言ったんだけ
ど、来る前に買い物に行くって言うから、家に戻って外で待ってたの。そ
したら、ちょうどあの方の乗った馬車が通りをやって来るのを見たのよ！」

　「わかった！　支度だ！」と父は言った。
　父は火に水をかけて消し、家中のただ一つのいすの座面を蹴り飛ばして
はがした。この様子に、マリウスはショックを受けた。テナルディエは妻
に、ベッドに行って病気のふりをしろといった。それから下の娘に、窓の
ガラスを割るように言った。

マリウス　　99

"But, father," said the little girl, "I'm afraid."

"Do it, now! Make yourself useful!" yelled the father.

The little girl was more afraid of her father than of broken glass. She put her hand through the glass and cried out. Her hand was bleeding.

"Look what you did!" yelled the mother. "She's hurt herself!"

"Even better!" cried the father. He ripped his shirt to make a bandage for her. An icy wind came through the broken window.

Looking around, the father looked pleased.

"Perfect," he said. "Now we can receive the gentleman."

■make oneself useful 役に立つ　■put ~ through ～を…に突き通す　■come through 通り抜ける

「でもお父さん、怖い」と小さな女の子は言った。

「今やりなさい！ 役に立ってみせろ」と父は叫んだ。

小さな女の子は、割れたガラスより父の方が怖かった。彼女はガラスに手をつき通し、悲鳴を上げた。手から血が流れていた。

「そんなことをやらせるから。見てごらん！」と母は叫んだ。「けがをしちゃったじゃない！」

「なおさらいい！」と父はわめき、自分のシャツを割いて娘に包帯を作ってやった。破れ窓から寒風が吹き込んできた。

あたりを見回し、父は満足したようだった。

「完璧だ」と彼は言った。「さあ、あの方をお迎えしよう」

VII

There was a knock, and Thénardier opened the door. To Marius's great shock, there stood Mademoiselle Black and Monsieur White!

"Thank you so much for coming!" said Thénardier as he welcomed his guests. "You see, we are desperate. We have no fire, and it is cold. Our only chair is broken, my wife is sick in bed, and my youngest hurt her hand at the factory where she works. Now she cannot work, so what will we do? We owe a year's worth of rent..."

Marius knew this was not true because he had already paid six-months' worth for them. But Thénardier went on, listing the family's various miseries.

"I see," said Monsieur White as Mademoiselle Black put a large package on the table. "That package contains some clothes, blankets, and stockings. I hope this will help for now, but I see your situation requires more."

■to one's shock 驚いたことに   ■sick in bed 病気で寝ている   ■go on 〜し続ける
■I see なるほど、わかりました   ■for now ひとまずのところは

VII

　扉をノックする音が聞こえて、テナルディエは扉を開けた。マリウスは
仰天した。マダモアゼル・ブラックとムッシュ・ホワイトだ!

　「ようこそお越しくださいました」とテナルディエは客人を迎え入れた。
「ご覧のとおり、どうしようもない有様でして。火もなく、凍えています。
一つしかないいすも壊れて、妻は病気で寝込みました。一番下の娘は、勤
め先の工場で手にけがをして、もう働けません。私たちにはどうすること
もできません。家賃も一年分滞納していて……」

　マリウスは一家に代わって6か月分の家賃を立て替え払いしていたの
で、この言葉が嘘だとわかっていた。でも、テナルディエは続けて、家族
の不幸をあれこれと言い立てた。
　「わかりました」とムッシュ・ホワイトは言い、マダモアゼル・ブラック
はテーブルの上に大きな包みを置いた。「この包みには、服や毛布やストッ
キングが入っています。これで当座はしのげると思うのですが、この状況
では、もっと必要なようですね」

マリウス　103

"You are too kind," said Thénardier.

"I only have five francs in my pockets now," said Monsieur White. "Let me take my daughter home. I will come back in the evening at eight o'clock."

Thénardier agreed and the two guests left.

Marius barely knew what to think, but he was overjoyed to see his Mademoiselle Black again. However, he still didn't know her name, or where she lived! Perhaps if he kept watching, he would find something out, he thought.

At eight o'clock, Monsieur White came back with more money as he had promised, and Marius was back at the hole in the wall, watching. But the daughters were not there, the wife was now out of bed, and several strange men entered the room after Monsieur White.

"Do not mind them," Thénardier told Monsieur White. "They are just a few friends of mine."

Suddenly, as Monsieur White placed several hundred francs on the table, Thénardier grabbed his hand.

"Don't you recognize me?" he yelled. "My name is Thénardier! I'm the innkeeper at Montfermeil."

■take someone home (人を)家まで送る　■find something out なにかしらを発見する　■keep doing ～しつづける

「なんともご親切に」とテナルディエは言った。

「今ポケットには5フランしか入っていないのです」とムッシュ・ホワイトは言った。「娘を家まで送らせてください。晩の8時に戻ってきます」

テナルディエは承知し、二人の客人は出て行った。

マリウスはどうにも考えがまとまらなかったが、マダモアゼル・ブラックに再び会えて有頂天だった。でも、名前も知らないし、どこに住んでいるかも知らないのだ！　ひょっとすると、のぞき見を続けていたら何かがわかるかも、とマリウスは思った。

8時になり、ムッシュ・ホワイトは約束通りもっと多くの金を携えて戻ってきた。マリウスは壁の穴の後ろに陣取って見つめていた。しかし、娘たちは居合わせず、妻はベッドから起き上がっていた。見知らぬ男が数人、ムッシュ・ホワイトの後に続いて部屋に入って来た。

「気にしないでください」とテナルディエはムッシュ・ホワイトに言った。「友人です」

ムッシュ・ホワイトが数百フランをテーブルの上に置くと、テナルディエは突然、ムッシュ・ホワイトの手をつかんだ。

「俺のことがわからないのか」とテナルディエはわめいた。「俺はテナルディエ！　モンフェルメイユの宿の主人だ」

Monsieur White stared at the man and looked all around the room. There were now seven dirty, rough-looking men in the room, yet Monsieur White seemed calm.

"No," he replied.

"You don't know me? Well I knew you as soon as you walked in here! You are the man who came to my inn eight years ago and took Fantine's child! You, dressed like a poor man, you are rich! You are fake, and you took away our help! You child-stealer!"

"I don't know what you mean. I'm not rich; I just try to give what I can. You must have me mistaken for somebody else."

Then, suddenly, Monsieur White shook Thénardier off his arm, jumped to the window, and was almost out of it before the men in the room grabbed him and pulled him back.

"I see now that you are bandits!" said Monsieur White as the men held him. "I gave you money; what else do you want from me?"

"What I need from you is 200,000 francs," said Thénardier. "I know you have it."

He went to the table where a knife lay under a cloth. He grabbed the knife and came close to Monsieur White.

■yet 腰 それにもかかわらず ■as soon as 〜するやいなや ■dress like 〜のような身なりをする ■somebody else 他の誰か ■come close to 〜に近づく

ムッシュ・ホワイトは男を見つめ、部屋中を見まわした。小汚い、屈強
そうな男が部屋に7人いた。でも、ムッシュ・ホワイトは落ち着いていた。

　「いいえ」とムッシュ・ホワイトは答えた。
　「俺のことを知らないのか。はん、お前がここに入って来た時から、お前
のことはわかっていたさ。8年前に俺の宿にやってきて、ファンティーヌ
の子を連れて行った男だろう。お前は貧しい身なりをしていたけど、実は
金持ちじゃないか。このペテン師め。俺たちの手伝いを連れていきやがっ
て。子さらいめが」
　「何をおっしゃっているのかわかりません。私は金持ちではないし、ただ
できるかぎりのことをして差し上げようと思ったのです。誰かほかの人と
お間違えではありませんか」
　突然、ムッシュ・ホワイトはテナルディエの腕を振り払って窓へと飛び
移り、外へ出ようとしたが、部屋にいた男たちが取り押さえて引き戻した。

　「お前たちはならず者だな！」とムッシュ・ホワイトは男たちに取り押さ
えられながら言った。「金は渡しただろう。ほかに何がほしいというのだ」

　「20万フラン必要だ」とテナルディエは言った。「持っていることはわかっ
ている」
　テナルディエはテーブルに向かった。布の下にはナイフがあり、テナル
ディエはそのナイフをつかんでムッシュ・ホワイトの近くにやって来た。

マリウス　107

"If you do not give me what I want, I can do bad things to that 'daughter' of yours," he said.

Just then, there was a great crash behind them. Marius shifted his view to see the other side of the room. The door had been broken open, and a tall man was standing there with a crowd of police behind him.

It was Inspector Javert.

"Just as I thought!" cried Javert. "I've been watching this room for bandit activity. You're all under arrest!"

A dozen policemen rushed into the room and arrested the bewildered bandits. But in the commotion, they neglected to arrest one man who slipped out unnoticed through the window. Upon seeing the police, Monsieur White had disappeared.

■break open こじ開ける ■under arrest 逮捕されて ■rush into 〜に突入する
■neglect to 〜し忘れる ■slip out こっそり抜け出す

「私の要求にこたえないならば、お前の『娘』とやらが危うくなるぞ」と彼は言った。

　ちょうどその時、男たちの背後で大きな物音がした。マリウスは部屋の反対側に視線を移した。扉はこじ開けられて、警察官の一団の前に背の高い男が立っていた。

　ジャヴェール警視だった。

　「思った通りだ」とジャヴェールは叫んだ。「犯罪行為が行われているとみてこの部屋を見張っていたんだ。お前たちを全員逮捕する！」

　十数人の警官が部屋に突入し、まごつくならず者たちを逮捕した。しかし騒動の間に、一人の男が誰にも気づかれることなく、窓からこっそりと抜け出したのを警官たちは見落としていた。警察を見るやいなや、ムッシュ・ホワイトは姿を消したのだ。

マリウス　109

確かな読解のための英語表現［文法］

would

助動詞wouldはさまざまな使われ方をします。かなり英語が読める人でもさらっと流して読んでしまうこともありがちな助動詞ですが、実はいろいろな意味、語法、ニュアンスを持っています。willが時制の一致で過去形になった場合、過去の習慣、同じく過去の強い意志、仮定法での用法など、軽くおさらいしてみましょう。

After her death, Monsieur Gillenormand decided that he would raise Marius.（p.74, 2行目）
娘の死後、ジルノルマンは自らマリウスを育てることにした。

【解説】that節内はもともとhe will raise Marius. という文ですが、主節の動詞、decideが過去形のかたちを取っているのに伴ってwillが過去形になっています。willという単語は、名詞では「意志」という意味があるように、助動詞のwillにも強い意志を表す場合が多く見受けられます。ここは主節の動詞、decide（決心する）という語と、時制の一致を受けたwouldからも、自分がマリウスを育てるのだ、というジルマルノンの強い決意が伝わってくる文です。

I told him to follow me, but he said he would go shopping before he came.【時制】（p.98, 7行目）
私について来てって言ったんだけど、彼は来る前に買い物に行くと言った。

【解説】これも動詞sayがsaidと過去形を使ったことから、willがwouldになった文です。he will go shopping（彼は買い物に行く）の文が、saidという動詞の過去形に引っ張られてhe would go shoppingとなりました。

また、最初のI told him to follow meは、「tell+人（を表す目的語）＋to不定詞〜」のかたちで「人に〜するように言う」という意味で、I told him that he would follow meと書き換えることができます。

110

When he saw his son here every week, he would weep.
（p.78, 一番下）

父親は毎週この場所から息子を見て泣いていました。

【解説】このwouldは過去の習慣的行為を表します。個人的な回想によく用いられ、特に物語文に多い用法です。また、過去の習慣的行為を表す語はほかにused toがありますが、こちらは過去の規則的な習慣について使用され、不規則な習慣はwouldで表します。この3文前にa man who was separated from his son used to come here every Sunday and hide behind this pillar to see his son.（息子から引き離された男が毎週この教会に来て、この柱の陰から息子の様子をうかがっていたのです）と記されていますが、こちらは毎週（日曜日）教会に行くという規則的な習慣を表しているためused toが使われています。

But the grandfather thought the man was a traitor and would not let him near the boy. （p.80, 5行目）

でも、祖父はその男のことを裏切り者と決めつけて、息子の傍に近づけなかったのです。

【解説】このwouldは過去の強い意志を表し「どうしても～しようとしなかった」という意味を持ちます。使役動詞letの前にwould notが置かれており「彼をその少年にどうしても近づけようとしなかった」と、強い拒絶を示しています。

Back at home, Mademoiselle Gillenormand would wonder out loud to Monsieur Gillenormand, （p.82, 下から3行目）

家に戻ると、マダモアゼル・ジルノルマンはムッシュ・ジルノルマンに向かって、声高にたずねた。

【解説】このwouldも同じく過去の強い意志で、マダモアゼル・ジルノルマンが、マリウスがいったい何をしているのか訝しく思って、ムッシュ・ジルノルマンにたずねたことを表しています。

111

> Perhaps if he kept watching, he would find something out, he thought. (p.104, 8行目)
>
> ひょっとすると、のぞき見を続けていたら何かがわかるかも、とマリウスは思った。

【解説】一見仮定法過去の文に見えます。しかし、最後のhe thoughtがこの文の主節（動詞のかたちを決定する節）の働きをしていることに気づくことが大切です。ifからコンマまではif he keeps watching, he will find something out.（見続けていたら、何かを発見するだろう）が元の文であり、thoughtが過去形であるのを受けて時制の一致が適用され、keepがkeptに、willがwouldになったものです。よってこれは直説法の文であり、仮定法過去（過去の事実に反する仮定を表す）ではありません。動詞のかたちだけを見れば間違えやすいと言えますが、文脈をきちんと追えていれば、正しい読み方ができる文でもあります。

その他、wouldの代表的な用法として、丁寧な依頼と慣用的に使われる表現があります。ひとつずつ例文を挙げておきます。

【例文1】　Would you tell me your phone number?
　　　　　（電話番号を教えていただけますか？）

丁寧に依頼するときの表現で、時制は過去のかたちですが、表しているのは「現在」であることに注意してください。

【例文2】　I would like to go to the nice Italian restaurant.
　　　　　（素敵なイタリアンレストランに行きたいです）

would likeにto不定詞が続いて、「～したいと思う」という意味になることを覚えておきましょう。

Part IV:
The Rue Plumet
プリュメ街

I

Marius had witnessed the whole thing. He was shocked, but he was quick to take action. The next day, he moved out without leaving a new address. He went to live with his old college friend, Courfeyrac, who shared Marius's revolutionary ideas. Marius still walked in the Luxembourg hoping to see Mademoiselle Black, but he never saw her anymore. He was heartbroken. He had been so close to finding out who she was, but he had lost her, and now he didn't know where to look.

Then, one day in the Luxembourg, he ran into another woman from his past. It was Eponine. She had grown more wretched, but also, strangely more beautiful.

"Oh, Monsieur Marius! I've found you!" she said with joy. "I've looked for you for so long. You left and didn't say where you were going! But now I've found you—it makes me so happy. You look well. Oh, but you have a hole in your shirt! I will mend it for you."

■be quick to すぐに〜する ■move out 引っ越す ■run into 〜に出くわす
■make ~ happy 〜をうれしがらせる ■look well 元気そうに見える

I

　マリウスは一部始終を見ていた。衝撃を受けたが、急いで行動に移った。翌日、マリウスは新しい住所を知らせずにアパルトマンを引き払った。マリウスは大学時代の旧友クールフェラックの下に身を寄せた。クールフェラックは、マリウスの革命思想に共感していたのだ。マリウスは、マダモアゼル・ブラックに会えるのではないかと思って今でもリュクサンブール公園を歩いていたが、もはや彼女を見かけることはなかった。マリウスの心は失意に沈んでいた。彼女の身元がすんでのところで分かったのに、姿を見失ってどこを探せばいいのかもわからなかったのだ。

　それから、ある日リュクサンブール公園で、マリウスはもう一人の旧知の女性に出会った。エポニーヌだった。前よりも哀れな姿になっていたが、それでもなぜか、前よりも美しかった。
　「ああ、ムッシュ・マリウス！　やっと見つけたわ」とエポニーヌは喜んで言った。「ずっとあなたのことを探していたのよ。行き先も言わずにいなくなったでしょう。でも、見つけたわ。本当にうれしい。お元気そうね。ああ、シャツに穴が開いてる。繕いましょう」

プリュメ街　115

Marius said nothing.

At his cold reception, Eponine darkened.

"You don't seem happy to see me," she said sadly. "I suppose you found out my parents were arrested."

Marius still said nothing.

"But I know something that will make you glad!" Eponine said quickly, almost wildly. "I know where *she* lives. That pretty miss whose father is the philanthropist. They used to walk here, in the Luxembourg. You'd like to know where she lives, wouldn't you? I know you fancy her."

"Yes! Take me there!" said Marius, suddenly coming to life.

Eponine led the way as Marius followed her to Mademoiselle Black's house.

Along the way, Eponine turned to say, "No, you must not follow so closely. Fall back a few steps. A gentleman like you shouldn't be seen walking with a person like me."

■philanthropist 图慈善家 ■fancy 動好む ■come to life 生き返る ■along the way 道中で ■fall back 後ろへ下がる

116　Part IV: The Rue Plumet

マリウスは何も言わなかった。

　冷たい反応に、エポニーヌの表情は暗くなった。

　「私に会えてもうれしくなさそうね」とエポニーヌは悲しそうに言った。「私の両親が捕まったのをきっとご存じなのね」

　それでもマリウスは何も言わなかった。

　「でも、あなたの気分がよくなることを知っているの」とエポニーヌは頭に血が上ったかのように早口で言った。「私は、あの娘の住処を知っているわ。あの可愛らしいお嬢さん。お父様は慈善家ね。前はここリュクサンブール公園を二人で歩いていたわね。あの娘の住んでいるところを知りたいでしょう。あなたがあの娘を好きだって知ってるのよ」

　「そのとおりだ。連れて行ってくれ」とマリウスは突然息を吹き返したかのように言った。

　エポニーヌが先導し、マリウスは彼女の後についてマダモアゼル・ブラックの家にたどり着いた。

　道中、エポニーヌは振り返ってこう言った。「だめよ、そんなに近づいちゃだめ。二、三歩離れて。あなたのような紳士が、私のような者と歩いているのを見られてはいけないわ」

プリュメ街　117

II

After Cosette had finished her education at the convent, Jean Valjean had rented a kind of hidden house that had an entrance on one street, on the Rue Plumet, and another entrance without an address around the corner on the Rue de Babylone. This house and its garden were nestled into the street corner and completely walled off. Whenever they went out, Jean Valjean insisted that they went out the back way, which did not have an address. Ever since the day that he had found Javert posed as a beggar, Jean Valjean had always tried to keep their residence and identity hidden.

Sometime after Jean Valjean and Cosette moved to the hidden house, Cosette looked in the mirror and realized that she had become pretty. It was a total surprise to her, for it had happened almost overnight. At first it was rather uncomfortable, but she decided to make the best of it. She bought herself some nice clothes and accepted the fact that she was no longer a girl—she was a lady. It was about this time when Marius first saw her again at the Luxembourg.

■nestle into ～に落ち着いて横たわる ■wall off 壁で守る ■whenever 腰 ～するときはいつも ■total surprise まったくの驚き ■make the best of ～を最大限活用する

II

　コゼットが修道院での教育を終えると、ジャン・ヴァルジャンはプリュメ通りに入口が一つ、バビロン通りの角に住所を書いていない出入口がもう一つある隠れ家を借りた。家と庭は通りの角に位置していて、四方を壁に囲まれていた。出かけるときはいつも、住所を書いていない方の裏道の出口から出るようにジャン・ヴァルジャンは言った。乞食に扮したジャヴェールを見つけた日から、ジャン・ヴァルジャンはいつも住居や身元を隠そうとしていたのである。

　ジャン・ヴァルジャンとコゼットが隠れ家に移ってからしばらくたって、コゼットは鏡を見て、自分が美しくなったことに気づいた。まるで一夜のうちに変わったので、コゼットはびっくり仰天した。はじめはどうにも落ち着かなかったが、せっかくの美貌を最大限に活用することにした。自分のために素敵な服を買って、もう少女ではなく、淑女になったという事実を受け入れたのだ。この頃、マリウスがリュクサンブール公園でコゼットに初めて再会したのだ。

プリュメ街　119

Jean Valjean had noticed Marius in the Luxembourg. Before, when Cosette was just a schoolgirl, Jean Valjean had not minded this young man. He seemed too stiff and proper, but there was nothing particularly wrong with him. However, one day, he saw Marius look at Cosette in a way that only a man in love would look. And, to Jean Valjean's great surprise, Cosette looked back at the young man in the same way!

Jean Valjean started to despise the young man. It was silly, he knew, but he was jealous. That was the truth. It upset him that Cosette was always so eager to take their daily walk in the Luxembourg. It was as if she lived for nothing else. Although Jean Valjean knew that he was acting foolish, he stopped walking in the Luxembourg. Cosette did not ask any questions. He was relieved about this. However, he noticed that Cosette was sad. She did not laugh as she used to, and she seemed to become pale and quiet. This broke Jean Valjean's heart. After a few weeks, he asked Cosette if she would like to go to the Luxembourg again. She lit up and said with joy, "Oh, yes!" Jean Valjean felt guilty for having taken away her greatest pleasure.

■in a way that 〜というやり方で   ■be eager to しきりに〜したがる   ■nothing else 他にはなにもない   ■ask if 〜 would like 〜に…はどうかとたずねる   ■light up （顔色が）ぱっと明るくなる   ■feel guilty for 〜に罪悪感を持つ

ジャン・ヴァルジャンは、リュクサンブール公園にいるマリウスに気づいていた。コゼットがまだ女学生だった頃は、ジャン・ヴァルジャンはこの若者のことを気にも留めなかった。マリウスは堅物できちんとし過ぎているように見えたが、別段問題もなかった。でもある日、恋に落ちた男だけが投げかける視線でマリウスがコゼットを見ていることに、ジャン・ヴァルジャンは気がついた。そして、コゼットも同じようにこの若者を見返したことに愕然とした。

　ジャン・ヴァルジャンは、この若者を見下すようになった。馬鹿げたこととはわかっていたが、マリウスに嫉妬したのだ。それは紛れもない事実だった。日課となったリュクサンブール公園での散歩にいつもコゼットが行きたがるのを見て、ジャン・ヴァルジャンは内心穏やかではいられなかった。コゼットの生きがいは、マリウスに会うことだけのように見えた。ジャン・ヴァルジャンは、馬鹿なことをしているとわかっていながら、リュクサンブール公園での散歩をやめた。コゼットは何も聞かなかった。ジャン・ヴァルジャンは、内心ほっとした。でも、彼はコゼットが悲しんでいることに気づいた。前のようには笑わなくなり、顔は青ざめて黙りがちになった。ジャン・ヴァルジャンの心は痛んだ。数週間後、彼はコゼットに、またリュクサンブール公園に行きたいかとたずねた。コゼットの顔はぱっと明るくなり、「ええ、もちろん」と嬉しそうに答えた。コゼットの一番の喜びを奪ってしまったことに、ジャン・ヴァルジャンは良心の呵責を感じた。

They went to the Luxembourg that evening, with Cosette chatting all the way there.

However, when they arrived, the young man was not there. Cosette lost some of her cheerfulness, although she continued to chat to be a good companion to Jean Valjean.

The next day, Jean Valjean asked Cosette, "Would you like to go to the Luxembourg today?"

Cosette, with downcast eyes, said quietly, "No, thank you."

■all the way 道中ずっと　■with downcast eyes 目を伏せて

二人はその晩リュクサンブール公園に行った。コゼットは道すがらずっと話をしていた。

　でも、公園につくと、あの若者はいなかった。コゼットはジャン・ヴァルジャンの相手をよく務めようとして話し続けたが、少し元気がなくなった。

　次の日、ジャン・ヴァルジャンはコゼットに、「今日もリュクサンブール公園に行こうか」とたずねた。

　コゼットは伏し目がちに、「いいえ」と答えた。

III

One day, as Cosette was walking in the garden at her house, she sat down on a bench close to the iron gate that faced the street. She heard her maid call for her, so she went to the house and returned to the bench in a few minutes. Upon her return, she noticed a large stone that wasn't there before on the bench.

At first, Cosette felt a pang of fear. Who had been here? Was someone in the garden? But she realized it could have been placed by someone outside who stretched his or her arm between the bars of the gate. She picked up the stone and noticed a letter under it. There was no signature or date, but she knew instinctually who it was from and whom it was for. It was from that young man to her! It was a love letter!

■upon one's return 戻ってくると ■feel a pang of fear 恐怖にかられる ■stretch one's arm 腕を伸ばす ■pick up 拾う ■instinctually 副本能的に

III

　ある日、コゼットは家の庭を散歩して、通りに面する鉄の門のそばにある
ベンチに座っていた。メイドの呼ぶ声が聞こえたので家に向かい、二、三
分してまたベンチに戻った。戻ってくると、先ほどはベンチの上になかっ
た大きな石に気がついた。

　はじめ、コゼットは恐怖に襲われた。誰かここにいたの？　誰かが庭にい
たのかしら？　でも、外にいた人が門の横棒の間から腕を差し出して石を
置いた可能性もあることに気づいた。コゼットが石を拾い上げると、下に
手紙があるのに気がついた。署名も日付もなかったが、誰から来て、誰に
宛てた手紙か、コゼットにはピンと来た。あの若者から自分に宛てた手紙
だ！　恋文だ！

プリュメ街　125

Cosette read the letter breathlessly, and when she was done, she kissed the paper. She ran up to her room, locked the door, and spent the night reading and rereading the letter. It made her heart flutter and her face feel hot. The young man expressed how she made him feel, how he had fallen in love with her. She wondered how and when she would hear from this young man again.

It was Jean Valjean's habit to go out for a long walk in the evenings. That evening, when he went out, Cosette arranged her hair in the way that most became her and put on a nice dress. For what? She didn't know what she was doing or what she expected, but she went out to the garden and sat on the bench. After she had been sitting there a while in the moonlight, she felt a presence behind her. She turned to see the young man standing at the gate.

Cosette's heart raced, and she was even a little afraid, but she did not cry out. The young man began to speak.

■hear from ～から連絡をもらう　■arrange one's hair 髪を整える　■in the way that most become ～を最もよくするやり方で　■feel a presence 気配を感じる

126　Part IV: The Rue Plumet

コゼットは息を切らして手紙を読んだ。読み終わると、手紙にキスをした。部屋へと駆け上がり、扉を閉めて、その晩は手紙を幾度も読んで過ごした。心はときめき、顔は火照った。あの若者が、コゼットを見てどう思ったか、どんな風に恋に落ちたかが書かれていた。ああ、この人から次はいつどうやって便りが来るのだろう。

　ジャン・ヴァルジャンは、夕方に長い散歩に出かけるのを日課としていた。その晩、ジャン・ヴァルジャンが出ていくと、コゼットは一番似合う形に髪を整えて、いい服を着た。なぜだろう。自分が何をしているのか、何を期待しているのか、我ながらよくわからなかったが、ともかくコゼットは庭に出ていき、ベンチに腰掛けた。しばらく月夜に照らされて座っていると、後ろに人の気配を感じた。振り返ってみると、あの若者が門の所に立っていた。

　コゼットの心は高鳴った。少し怖くもあったが、大声は出さなかった。若者は話し始めた。

プリュメ街　127

"Pardon me, I know I shouldn't have come here. I shouldn't disturb you. But my heart will burst if I don't tell you how I feel. Do you recognize me? Do you remember the look you gave me in the Luxembourg one day? I have loved you ever since!"

Cosette felt weak, but also sublimely happy. Not knowing what she was doing, she reached for his hand through the gate and put it over her heart. The young man lit up.

"You love me too, then?"

Cosette let the young man into the garden, and there they talked. When they had finished telling each other everything about themselves, she asked him, "What is your name?"

"My name is Marius. And yours?"

"My name is Cosette."

■perdon me　ごめんなさい　■feel weak　力が抜ける　■reach for　〜に手を伸ばす
■put ~ over　〜を…の上に置く　■let ~ into　〜を…に入れる

128　Part IV: The Rue Plumet

「お許しください。ここに来るべきではないってわかってはいたんです。あなたの邪魔をしてはいけないって。でも、もし自分の思いを伝えなかったら、私の心は破裂してしまいます。私のことがわかりますか。いつの日だったか、リュクサンブール公園で私にほほえみかけてくれたのを覚えていますか。その時以来、私はあなたを恋い焦がれているのです」

コゼットは体の力が抜けるのを感じたが、この上なく幸せでもあった。無意識のうちに門の向こうに手を差し出して若者の手をつかみ、自分の胸に当てた。若者の顔は輝いた。

「では、あなたも私を愛してくださるのですか」

コゼットは若者を庭に招き入れて、話をした。お互いに自分のことをすべて話し終えると、コゼットは若者にたずねた。「お名前は何とおっしゃるの」

「私はマリウスです。あなたは」

「コゼットよ」

IV

The lovers were able to meet like this in the garden in the evenings for about six weeks. They were both in heaven. But one day, Cosette changed everything.

"I have to go away," she said. "My father has business and we must go live in England."

Marius felt his whole world shattering.

"No!" he cried. "You cannot!"

Then, feeling quite desperate, he added, "I cannot live without you. I will die if you go away."

"Marius," said Cosette, "come with us! You don't have anything holding you here. You can come to England too!"

"You know I can't do that, for I have no money!" Then an idea struck Marius and he pulled out his pocket knife. He began to carve something on the garden wall.

■go away 立ち去る　■feel desperate やけを起こす気分になる　■pull out ～を取り出す　■carve 動 刻む

IV

　恋人たちは、一か月半ほど、晩になるとこんな風に庭で落ち合った。二人は天にも昇る気持ちだった。しかしある日、コゼットがすべてを変えてしまった。

　「行かなければならないの」とコゼットは言った。「父の用で、イングランドで生活しなければならなくなりました」

　マリウスは、世界が崩れ落ちるように感じた。

　「だめだ！」とマリウスは叫んだ「行かないで」

　そして、やけになってこう付け加えた。「君がいなければ生きていけません。行ってしまうなら、私は死ぬつもりです」

　「マリウス」とコゼットは言った。「一緒に来てください！　あなたをここに引き留めているものは何もないはずよ。イングランドに一緒にくればいいのよ！」

　「できないことはわかっているでしょう。私にはお金がないのです！」でもそのとき、マリウスはある考えを思いつき、ポケットナイフを取り出した。庭の壁に文字を刻み始めたのだ。

プリュメ街　131

"This is my address," he said, "16, Rue de la Verrerie. If anything happens, you should know where I live. I have an idea. I will not come tomorrow as usual, but I will see you the evening after at nine o'clock."

"But what is your idea? Marius, please tell me so I can sleep tonight!"

"You will know later, but I promise you this now: Nothing will separate us."

With that, he left the garden, and Cosette found herself alone, wondering what Marius was thinking.

■find oneself alone 一人きりであることに気づく

「これが私の住所です」とマリウスは言った。「ヴェルリー通り16番地。何かあったら、これで私の家がわかるはずです。一つ思いついたことがあります。明日はいつものようには来ませんが、晩の９時過ぎにお会いしましょう」

「どんな思いつきなのですか。マリウス、どうぞ教えてください。そうでないと、眠れませんわ」

「後でわかりますよ。でも、今これだけは約束します。私たちを引き離せるものは何もありません」

こう言い残して、マリウスは庭を去った。一人残されたコゼットは、マリウスは何を考えているのだろうといぶかしんだ。

プリュメ街　133

V

The next day, Jean Valjean was taking a turn at twilight among the trees and shrubs in his garden. He was deeply troubled. Paris was not quiet: political troubles were rocking the city, and people were starting to talk of revolution. Police were starting to inquire into the occupations and identities of suspected revolutionaries throughout the city. It was not a good time to be in hiding. This, coupled with Jean Valjean's discovery of Cosette's love affair, had made him decide to move away from France for good. In less than a week, he hoped to be in England.

When he got close to the bench where Cosette held her secret meetings with Marius, he noticed something written on the wall:

"16, Rue de la Verrerie."

■take a turn 散歩する　■inquire into 〜を取り調べる　■couple with 〜と相まって　■love affair 恋愛関係　■move away from 〜から離れる　■in less than a week 一週間足らずで

V

　あくる日の黄昏時、ジャン・ヴァルジャンは庭の木々や低木の間を散歩していた。心は乱れていた。パリは平穏ではなかった。政争が町を揺さぶり、革命の話が出始めていた。警官たちは、革命家と思しき人々の職業や身元を嗅ぎつけ回りだした。身を隠すにはよい時ではない。コゼットの色恋沙汰を突き止めたこともあって、ジャン・ヴァルジャンはフランスを出て、金輪際帰ってこないことにした。一週間もしないうちに、イングランドに行くつもりだった。

　コゼットがマリウスと密会を重ねていたベンチに近づくと、ジャン・ヴァルジャンは、壁に何かが書かれていることに気づいた。

　「ヴェルリー通り16番地」

プリュメ街　135

It was a new marking—fresh plaster from the wall dusted the shrubs below. Suddenly, instinctually, Jean Valjean knew exactly what this address was, and what it meant. It could only be *he*, that young man who paraded around and stared at Cosette in the Luxembourg! He had come here, to his home, and Cosette had allowed him in! It was worse than Jean Valjean had suspected: Cosette must truly be in love with that young man.

As Jean Valjean peered through the iron gate, he saw a figure standing on the street just outside. It was a youth, perhaps—too small to be a man, too big to be a boy. The figure flung something over the wall and ran off into the falling darkness. A folded piece of paper landed at Jean Valjean's feet. He picked it up and opened it. There were only three words on it: "Leave this place."

Greatly disturbed, Jean Valjean folded the paper again and went back to the house. He didn't know who wrote the note or what it meant, but he knew there was no time to waste. He would take action now.

■know exactly what ~ is ～が何であるかはっきりと分かる　■parade around うろつきまわる　■peer through ～をのぞき込む　■fling 動 ～を放り投げる　■run off 走り去る　■there is no time to waste ぐずぐずしている暇はない

この文字は新しく刻まれたものだった。壁から新しい漆喰がパラパラと落ちて足元の低木を汚していたからだ。突然、直感的に、ジャン・ヴァルジャンはこの住所がどこで、どんな意味を持つかを正確に悟った。あの男しかいない。リュクサンブール公園でコゼットの周りをうろついてじろじろ見つめていた、あの若者だ。奴はここに、私の家に来たのだ。そして、コゼットは奴を中に入れたのだ！　ジャン・ヴァルジャンが思っていたより事態は悪化していた。コゼットは、あの男に本当に恋をしているにちがいない。

ジャン・ヴァルジャンが鉄の門をのぞき込むと、すぐ外の通りに人が立っているのが見えた。若者だ。たぶんそうだ。男性というには小さすぎるし、少年というには大きすぎる。その人物は、何かを壁の上から投げてよこして、迫りくる暗闇の中に走り去った。折りたたんだ紙がジャン・ヴァルジャンの足元に落ちた。彼は拾い上げて紙を開いた。記されていたのはわずか8文字である。「この場所から去れ」

大いに動揺したジャン・ヴァルジャンは、紙を再び折りたたんで、家に戻った。誰がどんなつもりで書いたのかはわからないが、もう猶予がないことははっきりした。今すぐ行動に移らなければならない。

The next evening, Marius came out of Monsieur Gillenormand's house in despair. It was the first time he had seen his grandfather in years. It had taken all the strength he had to enter that house with dignity, but he had done it, and he had spent the evening asking—no, pleading—for his grandfather's permission to marry Cosette. His grandfather had refused on all counts, and Marius was devastated. His great idea had been to get his grandfather's consent and to marry Cosette before her father could take her away to England. But the plan had failed.

For the rest of the night, Marius wandered around Paris feeling numb. Without Cosette, he felt life held nothing for him. With no money or connections with which he could marry Cosette and build a life together, there was nothing he could do—death was the best option for him.

Through his wanderings, he seemed to hear strange sounds in Paris. Coming halfway out of his sad meditations, he wondered now and again, "Are they fighting?"

■on all counts あらゆる点で　■get someone's consent （人の）同意を得る
■wander around ぶらぶらと歩く　■feel numb ぼうぜんとする　■option 選択
■come halfway 中頃までくる　■now and again 時折

次の日の晩、マリウスはムッシュ・ジルノルマンの家から気落ちして出てきた。何年かぶりに、祖父に会ったのである。威厳を保ってこの家に入るにはありったけの力を振り絞らなければならなかったが、何とか家の門をくぐり、コゼットと結婚する許しを祖父から得ようと一晩中説得を試みた。いや、懇願したというべきか。しかし祖父はにべもなく断り、マリウスは打ちのめされた。コゼットが父親にイングランドへと連れていかれる前に、祖父の同意をとりつけるというのがマリウスの思いついた妙案だったのだが、計画はとん挫してしまった。

　その後、マリウスは無力感に苛まれながらパリ中を歩き回った。コゼットがいなければ、人生は何の意味もないだろう。コゼットと結婚してともに生活を築き上げていく金もつてもなく、何もできることはなかった。死が最良の選択であるように思われたのだ。

　歩き回るうちに、パリの町に耳慣れない音が響き渡った。悲しい物思いから半分醒めて、マリウスは時おり「戦っているのだろうか」と思った。

プリュメ街　139

At nine o'clock, he found himself on the Rue Plumet, in front of Cosette's iron gate. He let himself into the garden, expecting to see Cosette waiting for him on the bench. But she was not there. He looked at the house. All the windows were dark and the shutters closed.

"Cosette?" he called out tentatively.

There was no answer, and he grew bold. He went up to the house and knocked on the door.

"Cosette!" he called. No answer.

In a panic, he cried out again, "Cosette!"

Still no answer. So it was settled. Cosette was gone.

Marius sat down on the steps in front of the door. He smiled sadly, his heart full of tenderness for the time he had shared with this woman who was now gone. He had no regrets, and he had had the happiest six weeks he had ever known. But now, with Cosette gone, there was nothing more for him but to die.

■tentatively 副試しに ■let oneself into ～の中へ入る ■grow bold 大胆になる

9時に、マリウスはプリュメ通りの、コゼットが住む家の鉄門の前にた
どり着いた。コゼットがベンチに腰掛けて待ってくれていると思って庭に
入ったが、コゼットはそこにはいなかった。彼は家を見た。窓はみな暗く、
雨戸が閉められていた。

　「コゼット？」とマリウスは試しに呼びかけた。
　答えはなかった。マリウスは大胆な行動に出た。家に近づき、扉をノッ
クしたのだ。
　「コゼット！」とマリウスは呼びかけた。答えはない。
　パニックに陥って、マリウスは再び声を張り上げた。「コゼット！」
　やはり答えはない。一巻の終わりだ。コゼットは行ってしまったのだ。
　マリウスは扉の前の階段に腰掛けた。悲しげに微笑む彼の心は、もう行っ
てしまったこの女性とともに過ごした甘美なひと時の記憶で満たされてい
た。悔いはない。人生で最も幸せな6週間を過ごしたのである。でも今や
コゼットはいない。マリウスは死ぬよりほかになかった。

プリュメ街　141

Suddenly he heard a voice at the iron gate.

"Monsieur Marius, is that you?"

Marius rose and saw a figure at the gate.

"Yes," Marius replied. He knew that voice.

"Your friends are expecting you at the barricade, in the Rue de la Chanvrerie."

Yes, that voice sounded rather like Eponine's. Marius rushed through the gate and saw somebody who appeared to be a young man disappear into the twilight.

■sound rather like 〜のように聞こえる　■rush through 〜を駆け抜ける

突然、鉄門の所で声がした。

「ムッシュ・マリウスかしら」

　マリウスは立ち上がり、門の所に人影を見た。

「ええ」とマリウスは答えた。その声には聞き覚えがあった。

「ご友人たちが、シャンヴルリー通りのバリケードであなたをお待ちですよ」

　そうだ、その声はエポニーヌのように聞こえた。マリウスは門を走り抜けて、若い男のような人影が薄闇に消えて行くのを目にした。

プリュメ街　143

VI

Meanwhile, at the barricade, the revolutionaries talked in low voices. A dim lamp lit the tables of the wine-shop that served as their headquarters. The lamp threw strange shadows on the great red flag—the sign of the revolutionary—hanging on the wall behind them. The street, and the great barricade they had built to protect it, was dark and silent.

Enjolras, the chief of the revolutionaries, was making his preparations.

"Gavroche," he called to a young boy. "You are small, and nobody will see you. Go out of the barricades and walk by the houses. Look around the streets and tell me what is going on out there."

"Yes, chief!" said Gavroche. "Small people are good for something too!"

■revolutionary 图革命家　■serve as ～としての機能を果たす　■throw a shadow 影を落とす　■chief 图上役　■what is going on 現在起きていること

VI

　その間、バリケードでは、革命家たちが声を潜めて話していた。薄暗いランプが、革命家たちのアジトとなったワインショップのテーブルを照らしていた。革命の象徴である大きな赤い旗が後ろの壁にかかっているが、その上にランプが奇妙な影を落としている。通りも、通りを防御するために築いた大きなバリケードも、暗く静まり返っていた。

　革命家たちのリーダーであるアンジョルラスは身支度を整えていた。

　「ガヴローシュ」とアンジョルラスは少年に呼びかけた。「お前は小さいから、誰にも気づかれないだろう。バリケードから出て、家のそばを歩け。通りを見回して、様子を教えてくれ」

　「わかったよ、リーダー」とガヴローシュは言った。「小さい方が役に立つこともあるんだぜ！」

プリュメ街　145

VII

As Marius walked toward the Rue de la Chanvrerie, he heard confused sounds—the sound of muskets firing, of distant yelling. But these sounds came rarely. It was a sign that the government was taking its time to gather its forces.

He walked toward the barricade like a man who had accepted his destiny. He had been called, and he must go. Soon, he arrived at the Rue de la Chanvrerie. He saw the great barricade, and the wine-shop where his comrades were. Through the window of the wine-shop, he saw the red flag. Here, Marius stopped, pausing for one moment before he accepted his fate. He thought of Cosette, like a dying man reflecting on the sweetest moments of his life. Suddenly, he heard someone singing an old, traditional folk song in the street.

■fire 動 発砲する　■take one's time to 時間をかけて〜する　■forces 名 軍隊
■accept one's destiny 運命を受け入れる　■reflect on 〜を回顧する

VII

　マリウスがシャンヴルリー通りに向かって歩いていると、銃声や遠くの叫び声が騒然と聞こえてきた。しかし、こうした音はめったに聞こえなかった。それは、政府が時間をかけて軍勢を集めている証拠だった。

　マリウスは運命を従容として受け入れ、バリケードに向かって歩いた。呼ばれたのだから、行かねばならない。まもなく、マリウスはシャンヴルリー通りに到着した。大きなバリケード、そして同志のいるワインショップが目に入った。ワインショップの窓越しに、赤い旗が見えた。ここでマリウスは立ち止まり、一瞬間をおいてから運命を受け入れた。死にゆく者が人生で最も甘美な瞬間を思い出すかのように、コゼットのことを思った。突然、誰かが古い昔ながらの民謡を通りで歌っているのを耳にした。

プリュメ街　147

Enjolras rushed out of the wine-shop.

"It is Gavroche," Enjolras cried to the other men. "He is warning us."

Soon, little Gavroche climbed over the barricade and said, "They are here!"

In a moment, they could hear the sound of rhythmic footsteps in the distance. The revolutionaries all grabbed their arms to prepare for battle. These fifty men would fight against thousands.

There was much less time than they expected—too soon, they heard the footsteps at the barricade. There was a pause. Everyone waited. In the still moment, a soldier called from the other side of the barricade, "Who's there?"

Casting one glance at his men, Enjolras turned to the barricade, lifted his musket, and cried out, "French Revolution!"

"Fire!" came the reply from the other side.

A bright flash washed the whole street in a blue light, and an explosion of bullets blasted the barricade. The street shook, and the red flag in the wine-shop fell.

■rush out of 慌ただしく～を出る ■in a moment すぐに ■fight against ～と戦う ■still moment 一瞬の静けさ ■cast a glance at ～をちらっと見る ■bullet 图 弾丸

アンジョルラスがワインショップから駆け出してきた。

「ガヴローシュだ」とアンジョルラスはもう一人の男に言った。「俺たちへの警告だ」

すぐに、ガヴローシュ少年はバリケードの上に登って言った、「奴らが来るぞ！」

次の瞬間、遠くから規則正しい足音が聞こえてきた。革命家たちはみな武器を手に取り、戦いに備えた。50人の同志が数千人を相手に戦うのだ。

思っていたよりも時間は全然なかった。あまりにも早く、バリケードの所で足音が響いた。音が止まった。皆が待った。一瞬静けさが支配した後、兵士がバリケードの向こうから呼びかけた。「そこにいるのは誰だ」

仲間に目配せして、アンジョルラスはバリケードに向かい、マスカット銃を持ち上げて叫んだ。「フランス革命！」

「撃て！」と反対側から答えがあった。

まぶしい閃光が通り一帯を青い光で染め、弾丸が炸裂してバリケードを揺るがせた。通りが揺れ、ワインショップの赤旗が落ちた。

"Comrades!" cried Enjolras. "Hold strong! Do not waste your gun powder until they enter the barricade!"

In mere moments, the first of the soldiers climbed over the top of the barricade. A brave comrade, Bahorel, fired, killing him, but a second soldier who had just crested the barricade shot Bahorel down. Another soldier sprang down onto Courfeyrac, Marius's college friend.

"Help!" yelled Courfeyrac, while another soldier ran at little Gavroche with his bayonet.

Suddenly, a bullet struck the soldier standing over Courfeyrac in the head, and another bullet sank into the breast of the soldier running at Gavroche. As they died, Courfeyrac and Gavroche turned to see who had saved them. It was Marius.

■hold strong しっかりしろ　■climb over ～を乗り越える　■spring down 飛び降りる　■stand over ～の前に立ちはだかる　■sink into めり込む　■run at ～を急に襲う

150　Part IV: The Rue Plumet

「同志よ！」とアンジョルラスは叫んだ。「しっかりしろ！　奴らがバリケードに入ってくるまで火薬を無駄にするな！」

瞬く間に、最初の兵士がバリケードの上に登った。勇猛な同志バオレルが狙撃して兵士を倒したが、バリケードの頂上に登った二番目の兵士がバオレルを撃った。別の兵士が、マリウスの学友クールフェラックの上へと飛び降りた。

「助けて！」とクールフェラックは叫んだ。別の兵士が銃剣を構えてガヴローシュに突進した。

突然、クールフェラックの上に立っていた兵士の頭を銃弾が襲い、もう一発の銃弾が、ガヴローシュに向かって突進していた兵士の胸に突き刺さった。二人の兵士が死ぬと、クールフェラックとガヴローシュは振り返って救世主の姿を見た。マリウスだった。

プリュメ街　151

VIII

Marius had entered the barricade with two pistols. Now that they were both spent, he threw them away and turned toward the wine-shop for more weapons. Just then, a soldier aimed at him, but a hand was laid on the muzzle of the soldier's musket. The soldier fired, and the bullet went through the hand instead of Marius. The wounded person fell, but Marius barely noticed as he rushed into the wine-shop.

Marius saw a keg of powder in a corner, picked it up, grabbed a torch, and climbed in the shadows to one extreme corner of the barricade. He looked down at his comrades who were fighting off the numerous soldiers dropping down from the barricade. On the other side of the barricade, Marius saw a whole regiment of soldiers filling the street. The attack had been faster and more severe than the rebels had expected. Marius knew his friends could not last for long.

■muzzle 图銃口　■go through 〜を通り抜ける　■extreme 形もっとも端の
■fight off 撃退する　■last for long 長く持ちこたえる

VIII

　マリウスはピストルを二丁持ってバリケードに入った。両方とも使い切ったので、彼はピストルを投げ捨て、さらに武器を求めてワインショップへと向かった。ちょうどその時、兵士がマリウスに狙いを付けたが、兵士が持つマスカット銃の銃口に手が置かれていた。兵士は銃を撃ち、弾丸はマリウスの代わりにその手を貫通した。負傷者は倒れたが、マリウスはワインショップへと急いでいたので、ほとんど気にも留めなかった。

　マリウスは火薬の入った小さなたるを店の隅で見つけて拾い上げ、たいまつをひっつかみ、バリケードの一番隅っこの暗がりによじ登った。そこから、バリケードから飛び降りてくる多くの兵士たちと戦う同志たちを見下ろした。バリケードの向こう側に、兵士の大群が通りを埋めつくしているのが見えた。反乱軍の予想よりも早く、厳しい攻撃が加えられていた。マリウスは、友人たちが長く持ちこたえられないことを悟った。

Just as the commander was pointing his sword at the barricade to yell "Fire!" again, everyone heard a thundering voice come from above:

"Be gone! Or I will blow up the barricade!"

They all looked up to see Marius standing on top of a wall, holding a torch above his head, his other arm wrapped around a keg of gunpowder.

Everyone looked at him in horror.

"Blow up the barricade, and you will blow yourself up also!" cried a soldier.

"And myself also," answered Marius. He lowered the torch toward the powder. But there was no longer anybody in the street. The soldiers, leaving their dead and wounded, fled and were lost in the night. The barricade was saved.

■blow up 吹き飛ばす ■wrap one's arm around 腕を～に回す ■in horror 恐怖
におののいて ■dead and wounded 死傷者

154　Part IV: The Rue Plumet

司令官が剣でバリケードを指して再び「撃て」と叫ぶと、上からとどろく
声を皆が耳にした。

「ここを立ち去れ！　さもないと、バリケードを吹き飛ばすぞ」
　皆が見上げると、マリウスが壁のてっぺんに立ち、一方の腕で頭上にた
いまつを掲げ、一方の腕を火薬だるに回しているのが見えた。

　その姿を見て、誰もが恐怖におののいた。
　「バリケードを吹き飛ばしてみろ、お前も吹き飛ぶんだぞ」と兵士が叫ん
だ。
　「ああ、私もだ」とマリウスは答え、たいまつを下ろして火薬に近づけた。
しかし、もう通りには誰もいなかった。兵士たちは死傷者を残して逃げ出
し、夜の闇に消えていった。バリケードは救われたのである。

プリュメ街　155

IX

The rebels celebrated Marius and declared him a chief of the revolution. His friends embraced him and thanked him for joining them. While the rebels cared for the wounded and cleared away the dead, Marius walked through the dark, crooked streets to look at the other, smaller barricades. These had been largely ignored by the government's soldiers, for the main point of conflict had been the great barricade. However, some of the reinforcements had been blown up, and there was rubble here and there. As Marius walked past one pile of broken stones, he heard a weak voice say, "Monsieur Marius!"

He looked down, and there, among the rubble, was a young man—no, a boy. Marius bent down to the figure and saw it was not a boy but a young woman dressed in men's clothes. It was Eponine!

■care for 〜を介抱する　■clear away 〜を片付ける　■walk past 〜の横を歩く
■bend down かがむ　■not 〜 but 〜ではなく…

IX

　反逆者たちはマリウスを称え、革命のリーダーであると宣言した。友人た
ちはマリウスを抱きしめ、加勢に感謝した。反逆者たちがけが人を手当て
し、死者を片づけているうちに、マリウスは暗く曲がりくねった通りを歩
き、ほかの小さいバリケードを見て回った。政府軍の兵士たちはほとんど
気に留めなかったようだ。というのも、主戦場は大きなバリケードだった
からだ。でも、補強部分の一部が吹き飛ばされて、がれきが散らばってい
た。マリウスが石片の山を通り過ぎると、か細い声が聞こえてきた。「ムッ
シュ・マリウス！」

　見下ろすと、がれきの間に、若い男がいた。いや、少年だった。マリウ
スがその人の下へとかがんでみると、少年ではなく、男物の服を見た若い
女性であることがわかった。エポニーヌだ！

プリュメ街　157

"What are you doing here?" cried Marius, taking her into his arms.

"I am dying."

Marius was too shocked to reply, but he saw that Eponine's hand had a big black hole in it, and her chest was bleeding as well.

"Oh, God! How were you wounded? Here, I will carry you to the wine-shop. They will dress your wounds."

"Did you see a hand stop the gun that was aimed at you?" asked Eponine weakly.

"Yes…"

"That was mine. The bullet passed through my hand, and it went out through my back. It's too late to dress my wounds. But you can care for me by sitting with me for a while."

"I will stay with you," said Marius, holding her head.

"Monsieur Marius, you thought me ugly, didn't you?"

Marius did not know what to say.

■take ~ into one's arms ～を腕に抱える　■as well 同様に　■dress one's wound 傷に包帯をあてる　■pass through 貫通する

「ここで何をしているのですか」とマリウスは叫び、エポニーヌを腕に抱えた。

「私はもうだめよ」

マリウスはあまりの衝撃に答えられなかった。でも、エポニーヌの手には大きな黒い穴が開き、胸からも血が流れているのをマリウスは目にした。

「おお、神よ。どうしてけがをしたのですか。さあ、ワインショップへと連れていきましょう。けがの手当てをしてくれますよ」

「あなたに向けられた銃を手が止めたのをご覧になりましたか」とエポニーヌは弱々しくたずねた。

「ええ……」

「あれは私です。弾丸が手を貫通して、背中を通り抜けていったんです。けがの手当てをするにはもう手遅れです。でも、しばらく私の横に座っていていただければ、気が休まりますわ」

「ここにいますよ」とマリウスは言い、エポニーヌの頭を抱えた。

「ムッシュ・マリウス、私のことを醜いとお思いでしたでしょう」

マリウスは、どう答えていいかわからなかった。

プリュメ街　159

"It's no matter. It's all my fault. I led you here to this battle. But I don't want to deceive you anymore. I have a letter for you in my pocket. Since yesterday. From the pretty miss. She told me to deliver it to you, but I kept it because I didn't want you to have it...Take it."

Trembling, Marius reached into Eponine's pocket and took the letter.

"Now, promise me one thing."

"What, Eponine?"

"Kiss my forehead when I die."

Eponine stared into Marius's eyes, half smiling.

"Do you know? I believe I was a little in love with you."

She smiled again and passed away.

■no matter 構わない ■reach into ～に手を突っ込む ■believe 動 ～だと思う
■pass away 息を引き取る

「いいんです。みんな私のせいですから。私があなたを、この戦いに連れてきたのです。でも、もうあなたを欺きたくはありません。私のポケットに、あなたに宛てた手紙があります。昨日の手紙です。かわいいお嬢さんからよ。あなたに渡すように頼まれたのですが、あなたの下に届いてほしくなかったから、渡さないでおいたの……どうぞお取りになって」

震える手で、マリウスはエポニーヌのポケットに手を入れて、手紙を取り出した。

「ねえ、一つ約束してください」

「何でしょう、エポニーヌ」

「私が死んだら額にキスしてね」

エポニーヌは、半ば笑いながらマリウスの目をのぞき込んだ。

「ご存じだったかしら。私はたぶん、少しだけあなたのことを好きだったの」

エポニーヌはまたほほえんで、息を引き取った。

プリュメ街　161

X

Marius kept his promise. He kissed Eponine's forehead, but then his thoughts turned to the letter in his hand. This is the way it is with young lovers. He opened the letter and read: "I'm sorry, my love! My father wants to leave immediately. Tonight we will be in the Rue de l'Homme Armé, No. 7. In a week we will be in England. Cosette."

What had happened was simple: Eponine had done it all. She had dressed in men's clothes. It was she who had given Jean Valjean the message to leave. Jean Valjean had taken heed and told Cosette that evening to pack her things; they would go stay at another house on the Rue de l'Homme Armé, and in a few days they would be in London.

■keep one's promise 約束を守る　■turn to 次に〜のことを考える　■take heed 用心する　■pack one's things 荷物をまとめる

X

　マリウスは約束を守った。エポニーヌの額にキスしたものの、その後マリウスの関心は、手に握りしめた手紙へと移った。若い恋人たちだから、致し方ないところだ。彼は手紙を開封して目を通した。「あなた、ごめんなさい！　お父様がすぐに出発したいと言うの。今晩はロム・アルメ通り7番地におります。一週間後にはイングランドに向かいます。コゼット」

　何が起こったかは火を見るより明らかだった。全部エポニーヌの仕業だ。男物の服を着て、ジャン・ヴァルジャンに立ち退くようメッセージを送ったのは彼女だ。ジャン・ヴァルジャンは重く見て、その晩のうちにコゼットに荷造りするように言ったのだ。二人はロム・アルメ通り沿いの別の家に移り、数日後にロンドンに行くことになった。

プリュメ街　163

Cosette, devastated by this news, had written to Marius in a hurry. But how would she get the letter to him? She never went out alone, and she could not send her maid. This was when Cosette looked through the gate and saw a youth on the street. It was Eponine, who had been prowling around Cosette's street all evening, hoping that this exact thing would happen. Cosette gave the "youth" five francs and asked him to deliver the letter to 16, Rue de la Verrerie. Eponine put the letter into her pocket.

The next day, Eponine went to Courfeyrac's house not to deliver the letter, but just to see Marius. But Marius was not there, and Courfeyrac told her that all his comrades were going to the barricades that night. She had an idea: she would throw herself into death, and Marius along with her. That evening she went to Cosette's house, where she knew she would find Marius. She knew he would be devastated to find Cosette gone. She told him that his friends were waiting for him at the barricade, and, having nothing left to live for, he had followed her. But, her love for him proved too great to let him die.

■prowl around うろつきまわる ■put ~ into ～を…にしまう ■throw oneself into death 死の淵に身を投げる ■have nothing left to live for 生きがいが何もない ■let ~ die ～を死なせる

コゼットはこの知らせに打ちひしがれて、マリウスに急いで手紙を書いた。しかし、この手紙をどうやって届ければいいのだろう。一人で外に出たことなど一度もなかったし、メイドを遣わすこともできなかった。コゼットが門の向こうを見やり、通りに若者の姿を見かけたのはこの時だ。エポニーヌだ。事態がまさにこうなるようにと願いながら、一晩中コゼットの家のある通りのあたりをうろついていたのだ。コゼットは「若者」に5フラン渡し、手紙をヴェルリー通り16番地に届けるように頼んだ。エポニーヌは手紙をポケットにしまった。

翌日、エポニーヌはクールフェラックの家に行った。手紙を渡すわけではなく、ただマリウスに会いに行ったのだ。でもマリウスはそこにはおらず、クールフェラックはエポニーヌに、同志たちがその晩バリケードに集う予定だと言った。エポニーヌはある企みを思いついた。自分も死の淵に身を投げて、マリウスも道連れにしようというのだ。その晩、エポニーヌはコゼットの家に行った。そこにいけばマリウスに会えることはわかっていた。コゼットが行ってしまい、マリウスが落胆していることはわかっていた。エポニーヌはマリウスに、友人たちがバリケードの所で待っていると言い、生きがいをすべて失ってしまったマリウスは、エポニーヌの後を追った。しかしエポニーヌはマリウスをあまりにも愛していたので、ただ死なせることはできなかったのだ。

プリュメ街　165

Marius now had Cosette's letter, but nothing had changed. He still could not marry her, and she would still go to England. In a hurry, he wrote this letter from a sheet in his notebook:

"My grandfather has refused our marriage, and neither of us have money to start our lives together. I ran to your house, but you were already gone. Now, I go to die, but I will keep my promise to you that nothing will separate us. I will never be far from you. When you read this, my soul will be near you, smiling upon you."

He found Gavroche and told him to take the letter to Mademoiselle Cosette, Rue de l'Homme Armé, No. 7.

Gavroche left right away so that he could return to the barricade sooner. When he arrived at Rue de l'Homme Armé, he found an older man with white hair sitting outside. It was Jean Valjean, deep in thought.

"Does a Mademoiselle Cosette live here?" asked Gavroche.

"Yes, who wants to know?" replied Jean Valjean with suspicion.

■neither of どちらも〜でない ■far from 〜から離れて ■smile upon 〜にほほえむ ■right away すぐに ■deep in thought じっと考え込んで

マリウスはコゼットの手紙を読んだが、事態は何も変わっていなかった。コゼットとは結婚できないし、コゼットがイングランドに行ってしまうことに変わりはない。取り急ぎ、マリウスはノートの一頁に手紙を書いた。

「祖父は私たちの結婚を認めてくれず、二人とも新しい生活を始めるだけの金はありません。あなたの家に駆けつけたのですが、もうあなたはいなくなっていました。これから私は死地に赴きますが、私たちを分かつものは何もないという約束を守ります。あなたのそばを離れることは絶対にありません。あなたがこの手紙を読むとき、私の魂はあなたの近くにいて、あなたにほほえんでいるのです」

マリウスはガヴローシュを見つけて、手紙をロム・アルメ通り7番地のマダモワゼル・コゼットに届けるよう頼んだ。

ガヴローシュはバリケードにすぐ戻ってこれるように、すぐに出かけた。ロム・アルメ通りに着くと、白髪の老人が外に座っているのを見つけた。ジャン・ヴァルジャンが考えに沈んでいた。

「マダモワゼル・コゼットはこちらにお住まいですか」とガヴローシュはたずねた。

「そうだ。君は誰だね」とジャン・ヴァルジャンは疑い深そうに答えた。

プリュメ街　167

"I have a letter for her from Monsieur Marius, a comrade of the revolution!" said little Gavroche.

Jean Valjean's eyes narrowed.

"I will take the letter to her," said Jean Valjean. But instead, when Gavroche had gone, he opened the letter and read it.

■take ~ to ～を…に届ける　■instead 副 その代わりに

「革命の同志ムッシュ・マリウスから手紙を預かっているのです」とガヴ
ローシュ少年は言った。

　ジャン・ヴァルジャンは、眉をひそめた。

　「その手紙をコゼットに届けましょう」とジャン・ヴァルジャンは言った。
しかし、ガヴローシュが行ってしまうと、ジャン・ヴァルジャンは、手紙
を開けて中身を読んだ。

プリュメ街　169

確かな読解のための英語表現 ［文法］

：（コロン）と ；（セミコロン）

今回は句読点法を扱います。日本語の句読点記号に意味があるように、英語のこうした記号もそれぞれ意味を持っています。：（コロン）や ；（セミコロン）、―（ダッシュ）は単なる文の飾りではありません。記号が持つ意味をきちんと把握して英文を読むと、細かいニュアンスまではっきりとわかるようになります。

> "You will know later, but I promise you this now: Nothing will separate us."（p.132, 下から4行目）
> 「後でわかりますよ。でも、今これだけは約束します。私たちを引き離せるものは何もありません」

【解説】コロンは、前に述べたことについて具体例や説明などを付け加えるときに用います。この前までは大まかな説明で、コロンの後に細かい情報が続くことになります。ここでは「このことを約束します」の後にコロンがきており、細かい約束の内容（何物も私たちを引き離すことはない）が述べられています。

> Paris was not quiet: political troubles were rocking the city, and people were starting to talk of revolution.（p.134, 3行目）
> パリは平穏ではなかった。政争が町を揺さぶり、革命の話が出始めていた。

【解説】ここも同じように、「パリは平穏ではなかった」という概要説明の後にコロンがあり、その後に具体的にどんな様子であったのかが述べられています。

170

When he got close to the bench where Cosette held her secret meetings with Marius, he noticed something written on the wall: "16, Rue de la Verrerie." (p.134, 下から4行目)

コゼットがマリウスと密会を重ねていたベンチに近づくと、ジャン・ヴァルジャンは、壁に何かが書かれていることに気づいた。「ヴェルリー通り16番地」

【解説】この文では、「壁に何かが書かれていた」という説明をしておいたあとにコロンが来ており、壁に書かれていた具体的な内容がここに記されています。慣れてくると、コロンの前まで来たところで、次には、何が書かれていたのかが来るのだろうと予測できるようになります。このように予測読みができるようになると、英文を読むのもずっと楽しく、また速くなります。

He opened the letter and read: "I'm sorry, my love! My father wants to leave immediately." (p.162, 3行目)

彼は手紙を開封して目を通した。「あなた、ごめんなさい！ お父様がすぐに出発したいと言うの」

【解説】コロンの前までは、マリウスが手紙を開封して、それを読んだと記されており、このコロンがあることによって、次に手紙の具体的な内容がくるだろうと予測できます。前の例と同じで、どこかに何かが書かれているという情報をまず提起したうえで、コロンの後で具体的な内容がきています。

It was worse than Jean Valjean had suspected: Cosette must truly be in love with that young man. (p.136, 6行目)

ジャン・ヴァルジャンが思っていたより事態は悪化していた。コゼットは、あの男に本当に恋をしているはずだ。

【解説】この文の主語は、状況を表すitと呼ばれ、漠然と状況を指しています。コロンの後には、「どのような状況なのか」が具体的に描写されています。

What had happened was simple: Eponine had done it all.
（p.162, 下から6行目）

何が起こったかは火を見るより明らかだった。全部エポニーヌの仕業だ。

【解説】最初のwhatは関係代名詞であり、what had happenedで「起こったこと」という意味になります。何が起こったのか、どういうことだったのかがわかった。すべてはエポニーヌがしたことだったのだ、という説明がコロンに続いて語られています。

Jean Valjean had taken heed and told Cosette that evening to pack her things; they would go stay at another house on the Rue de l'Homme Armé, and in a few days they would be in London. （p.162, 下から4行目）

ジャン・ヴァルジャンは重く見て、その晩のうちにコゼットに荷造りするように言ったのだ。二人はロム・アルメ通り沿いの別の家に移り、数日後にロンドンに行くことになった。

【解説】日本人の英語学習者にとって意味が取りづらい記号にセミコロンがあります。コンマよりもはっきりと前後の節を分け、ピリオドよりはつながりを持たせる働きを持っています。ここでは、最初の節で荷造り、次の節で引っ越しについて述べられており、ピリオドで明確に分けるよりも2つの節が強いつながりをもっているため、セミコロンが使われています。

I'm not rich; I just try to give what I can. （p.106, 10行目）

私は金持ちではないし、ただできるかぎりのことをして差し上げようと思ったのです。

【解説】これも、私は金持ちではない、（だが）できる限りのことをしてあげたいという内容の2つの節を、ピリオドではなく、セミコロンで結ぶことで、相関性を高めています。

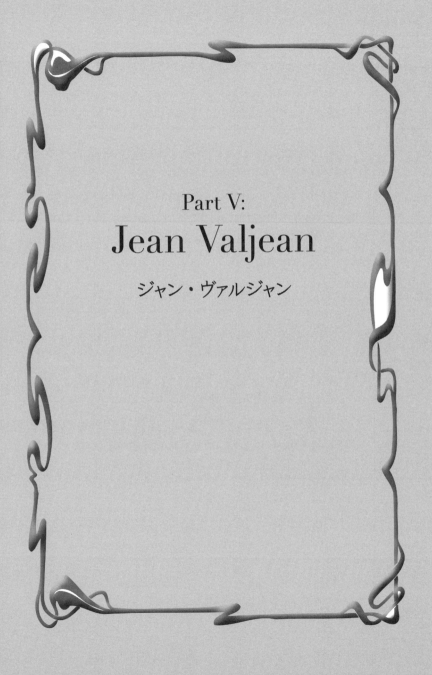

Part V:
Jean Valjean

ジャン・ヴァルジャン

I

After he had read the letter, Jean Valjean sat still for a long time, thinking. He felt joy—this young man who wanted to take Cosette away was going to die! He would never have to worry about him anymore and Cosette would be safe. But at the same time...He thought about how happy Cosette had been every time they walked in the Luxembourg...

Silently, Jean Valjean put on his coat, went out, bought a gun, and made his way to the barricade.

When Jean Valjean arrived at the rebels' headquarters, he immediately spotted Marius. The young man looked grim, and strong, and hardened. He also saw the little boy who had delivered Cosette's letter. He was pointing to a tall man seated in a dark corner of the wine-shop. Jean Valjean recognized that tall man.

■sit still じっと座っている　■never have to ～する必要がない　■at the same time その一方で　■make one's way to ～に向かって進む　■spot 翻見て～に気付く　■look grim 険しい表情をしている

I

　手紙を読むと、ジャン・ヴァルジャンは、腰掛けたまま、長い間考えに
ふけっていた。彼は喜びを覚えた。コゼットを奪い去りたいと思っていた
この若者は、死のうとしているというのだ！　マリウスのことは二度と思い
煩う必要もなく、コゼットは無事だろう。でも一方で……リュクサンブー
ル公園で一緒に散歩をしていたとき、いつもコゼットがどんなに嬉しそう
だったかを思い出していた。

　黙ったまま、ジャン・ヴァルジャンは外套を着て外出し、銃を買って、バ
リケードへと向かった。
　反逆者たちのアジトに着くと、ジャン・ヴァルジャンはすぐにマリウスを
見つけた。険しい顔をしたマリウスは、腕っぷしが強く、鍛え上げられて
いる様子だった。また、コゼットの手紙を届けてくれた男の子も目に入っ
た。ガヴローシュ少年は、ワインショップの暗い片隅に腰掛けた背の高い
男を指さしていた。ジャン・ヴァルジャンは、その男に見覚えがあった。

"Chief," the boy was saying to one of the rebels, "that man there is a spy."

Enjolras studied the man closely and nodded. Enjolras motioned to three other large men, and they all approached the tall man in the corner.

"Who are you?" Enjolras asked. This direct question may have startled a normal man, but the big man began to smile.

"You are a spy?" continued Enjolras.

"I am an officer of the government," he replied. "My name is Javert."

Enjolras made a motion to the three men, and in a moment they had searched Javert and tied him up.

"Spy," said Enjolras, "you will be shot before the barricade is overtaken."

"If I may," said a voice behind him, "I volunteer to kill the spy."

Everyone turned to see who had spoken. It was a large, older man with white hair. Marius recognized him immediately as Monsieur Fauchelevent, Cosette's father! Javert recognized him too, but as Jean Valjean, the convict.

■study ~ closely ～をよく調べる　■motion to ～に合図する　■startle 動 ～をびっくりさせる　■tie ~ up ～を縛り上げる　■If I may もしよろしければ

「リーダー」とガヴローシュは反逆者たちの一人に言った。「あそこにいる男はスパイだよ」

アンジョルラスはその男をよく見てうなずいた。アンジョルラスは他の三人の大男に合図し、男たちはみな、隅にいるその背の高い男に近づいた。

「お前は誰だ」とアンジョルラスはたずねた。こう単刀直入に聞くと、普通の男は驚くかもしれないが、この大男は笑みを浮かべ始めた。

「君はスパイなのか」とアンジョルラスは続けた。

「私は政府の役人だ」と彼は答えた。「ジャヴェールと言う名前だ」

アンジョルラスは三人の男に合図した。三人はただちにジャヴェールの身体検査をして縛りつけた。

「スパイよ」とアンジョルラスは言った。「バリケードが突破される前に、お前は銃殺だ」

「できれば、私にそのスパイを殺らせてほしい」と後ろから声がした。

声の主を探して皆が振り向いた。大柄な白髪の老人だった。マリウスはすぐに、ムッシュ・フォーシュルヴァンだと気づいた。コゼットの父親だ！ ジャヴェールも老人の正体に気づいた。罪人のジャン・ヴァルジャンだ。

"Very well," said Enjolras. "I entrust him to you."

Jean Valjean made Javert stand up and led him outside. He found a dark, hidden corner just beyond the barricade. He loaded his pistol as Javert watched him. And then—to Javert's shock—he untied him.

"You are free," said Jean Valjean.

Javert was not a person who was easily surprised. But the shock of this almost made him fall over.

"I don't expect to leave here alive," continued Jean Valjean, "but if I do, I live under the name Ultimus Fauchelevent. I stay at 7, Rue de l'Homme Armé."

Unable to find the words to speak, Javert slowly backed away, then wrapped his arms around himself and walked off, looking deeply troubled. When Javert had gone, Jean Valjean raised his pistol in the air and shot once. Then, he turned and walked back into the wine-shop.

■entrust ~ to ～を…に委ねる　■load a pistol ピストルに弾を込める　■not expect to まさか～するとは思わない　■leave ~ alive 生きて～を出る　■find a word to speak 言うべき言葉を探す　■back away 後ずさりする

「結構だ」とアンジョルラスは言った。「奴をあなたに託そう」

　ジャン・ヴァルジャンはジャヴェールを立たせて、外に行かせた。彼はバリケードのすぐ先に、薄暗く、人目につかない角地を見つけた。ジャヴェールが見ている前で、ジャン・ヴァルジャンはピストルに弾を込めた。それから、ジャヴェールが驚いたことに、ジャン・ヴァルジャンは彼の縄を解いた。

　「あなたは自由の身です」とジャン・ヴァルジャンは言った。

　ジャヴェールは、そうやすやすと驚く人間ではなかった。でも、あまりの驚きに卒倒しそうだった。

　「私はここを生きて出るつもりはありません」とジャン・ヴァルジャンは続けた。「でも、もし生き延びたら、私はユルティム・フォーシュルヴァンという名で、ロム・アルメ通り７番地に滞在しています」

　言うべき言葉が見つからず、ジャヴェールはゆっくり後ずさりし、両腕で自分の肩を抱え込んで歩き去った。大いに悩み苦しんでいる様子だった。ジャヴェールがいなくなると、ジャン・ヴァルジャンはピストルを空に向けて一発撃った。それから、彼は踵を返してワインショップへと戻った。

II

The sun soon came up, and by noon that day, the barricade fell. The heavy fighting left many dead, including Courfeyrac. Marius fought bravely, even with the cuts on his head bleeding into his eyes. As he fought, a bullet struck his shoulder. He fell fainting, but he felt a hand grab him. "I am taken prisoner," was his last thought.

But the hand that had grabbed him was not a soldier's. It was Jean Valjean's. He lifted Marius onto his back and, in the midst of the fighting, carried him from the great barricade down a crooked street. He disappeared around the corner of a house. There, amongst the rubble of a smaller barricade, he saw a hole in the ground with an iron grate over it—a sewer. The damage to the street had left the grate broken, and he could just squeeze himself and Marius down into the hole. This would be their escape. Still carrying the unconscious Marius, Jean Valjean disappeared into the sewer.

■fall 動 陥落する　■in the midst of ～の真っただ中　■sewer 名 下水道　■squeeze ~ into ～をぎゅうぎゅうと押し込む

II

　まもなく日が昇った。その日の正午頃には、バリケードは崩されてしまった。激しい戦闘で多くの者が命を落とした。クールフェラックも倒れた。マリウスは頭に切り傷を負い、目に血が流れ込んできたが、それでも勇敢に闘った。戦ううちに、銃弾がマリウスの肩に命中した。気を失いつつあったが、誰かの手が自分を握りしめるのを感じた。薄れゆく意識の中で、マリウスは最後に「敵の手に落ちるのか」と思った。

　しかし、マリウスをつかんだのは兵士ではなく、ジャン・ヴァルジャンの手だった。ジャン・ヴァルジャンはマリウスを背中に担ぎ、戦闘の最中にもかかわらず、マリウスを大きなバリケードから曲がりくねった通りへと運んだ。ジャン・ヴァルジャンは、ある家の隅のあたりで姿を消した。小さなバリケードのがれきの間に、鉄格子で覆われた穴が地面に開いているのを見つけたのだ。下水道だ。通りが損傷して鉄格子は壊れており、ジャン・ヴァルジャンはマリウスと自分の身を押し込んで穴の下にたどり着くことができた。これで逃れられる。意識を失ったマリウスを運びながら、ジャン・ヴァルジャンは下水道へと消えていった。

It took hours of walking through slime and filth with Marius on his back for Jean Valjean to reach the Grand Sewer. Once there, he could see light at one far end, and he knew there was an exit. He felt a great wave of relief, and he put Marius down to rest for a moment. Marius was still unconscious and losing more blood by the minute, but he was still breathing. Jean Valjean searched Marius's pockets. He found a notebook. Before the battle of the barricade, on the first page of the notebook, Marius had written, "My name is Marius Pontmercy. Carry my corpse to my grandfather's, Monsieur Gillenormand, Rue des Filles du Calvaire, No. 6."

As Jean Valjean rested, he pondered this. Then, with new resolve, he put Marius on his back again and made his way toward the exit. He didn't know someone had been watching him and following him through the sewers.

When he reached the exit, Jean Valjean discovered it was locked. He shook the iron bars of the grate but they wouldn't budge. He had made it this far, but there was no way out! He began to feel that it was all for nothing—that he and this young man would die here in the sewers. And then he thought not of himself, nor of Marius, but of Cosette.

■take hours of ～するのに数時間を要する　■far end 突き当り　■by the minute 刻々と　■with new resolve 決意を新たにして　■way out 出口　■all for nothing 無駄に

182　Part V: Jean Valjean

背中にマリウスを背負いながら、へどろや汚物の間を何時間も歩いて、ジャン・ヴァルジャンは大水路へとたどり着いた。ここまで来ると、遠い反対側の端に明かりが見え、出口があることがわかった。安堵の波が押し寄せ、ジャン・ヴァルジャンはマリウスを下ろして少し休んだ。マリウスはまだ意識がなく、刻々と血を失っていたが、それでも息はあった。ジャン・ヴァルジャンはマリウスのポケットを探り、ノートを見つけた。バリケードで戦闘が始まる前、ノートの最初のページに、マリウスはこう書いていた。「私の名はマリウス・ポンメルシーです。私の死体をフィーユ・デュ・カルヴェール６番地、祖父のムッシュ・ジルノルマンの家へと運んでください」

　ジャン・ヴァルジャンは休みながら、この言葉を反芻していた。そして決意を新たに、マリウスを再び背負って出口へと向かった。でも、自分のことを監視して、下水道を後からついて来ている人がいることには気づかなかった。

　出口に着くと、ジャン・ヴァルジャンは鍵が掛かっていることに気づいた。鉄格子の棒を揺さぶったが、びくともしない。はるばるここまでやって来たのに、出口がない！　すべてが無駄だったのではないかとジャン・ヴァルジャンには思えてきた。自分もこの若者も、下水道で朽ち果てるのだ。その時、彼は自分のことでもマリウスのことでもなく、コゼットのことを思っていた。

In the middle of his anguish, he heard a voice behind him.

"I have the key."

Jean Valjean turned to see a very thin, very dirty man holding a large key. And he knew the face of the man—it was Thénardier!

However, Thénardier didn't seem to recognize either Jean Valjean or Marius, covered as they were in wounds, blood, and sewer slime.

"I will let you out if you give me half of your earnings," said Thénardier.

"What do you mean?"

"It's clear you're an assassin. No one would carry a dead man through all these sewers unless you want to hide the body. I will let you out so you can hide the body, and I won't say anything about this to anyone. Just give me half of what you earned to kill this man."

Silently, Jean Valjean searched through his pockets for money. Meanwhile, Thénardier bent down and ripped a strip of cloth out of Marius's coat to report a murder—for a reward, of course—and to have something to show as evidence. Jean Valjean did not notice him doing this.

■not ~ either A or B　AもBも~ない　■let ~ out　~を外に出す　■no one would　誰も~しないだろう　■search through　~をくまなく探す　■strip of cloth　布きれ

184　Part V: Jean Valjean

苦しみの最中に、ジャン・ヴァルジャンは背後から声がするのを耳にした。

「俺は鍵を持っている」

ジャン・ヴァルジャンは振り返り、痩せこけた、汚らしい男が大きな鍵を持っているのを見つけた。その男の顔には見覚えがあった。テナルディエだ！

しかし、テナルディエは、ジャン・ヴァルジャンにもマリウスにも気づかなかった。二人とも傷だらけで血や下水のへどろにまみれていたからだ。

「稼ぎの半分をくれたら、外に出してやるよ」とテナルディエは言った。

「どういうことだ」

「お前が暗殺者なのは分かっている。死体を隠したいのでなければ、こんな下水道を通って死んだ男を運ぶわけがない。外に出て死体を隠させてやろう。他の誰にも、このことは言わない。ただ、この男を殺して稼いだ金の半分を俺によこせばいい」

ジャン・ヴァルジャンは黙ってポケットをまさぐり、金を探した。一方、テナルディエはかがんでマリウスのコートから布の切れ端を破りとった。人殺しを通報して、証拠品を提示するためである。もちろん、報奨金を得たい一心からだ。ジャン・ヴァルジャンは、テナルディエの仕業には気づかなかった。

After much searching, Jean Valjean came up with only thirty-two francs.

"You didn't kill him for very much, did you?" said Thénardier, and he took all the money instead of half.

Thénardier opened the gate as Jean Valjean picked up Marius again. As soon as they were out, Thénardier slammed the gate shut, locked it, and disappeared back into the sewers.

■come up with 〜を工面する　■slam 〜 shut 〜をバタンと閉める

あちこち探したが、ジャン・ヴァルジャンは32フランしか見つけられな
かった。

　「ずいぶんなはした金でこいつを殺したんだな」とテナルディエは言い、
半分ではなく全部を奪い取った。

　ジャン・ヴァルジャンがマリウスを再び背負うと、テナルディエは門を
開けた。二人が外に出るやいなや、テナルディエは門をバタンと閉めて鍵
をかけ、再び下水道へと消えていった。

III

They were outside! At Jean Valjean's feet was a little river, the water of which fed into the sewer. Jean Valjean stooped before the river, let Marius down, and poured a handful of water onto Marius's face. As he was involved in this task, he felt a presence approach him. He looked up. It was Javert!

"Jean Valjean," said Javert grimly as he grabbed the ex-convict by the shoulders.

"Inspector Javert," he said, "I am your prisoner. I gave you my address last night so that you could find me if I lived. I'll go with you willingly, but please help me do one thing. Help me take this young man, who is dying, to his grandfather's house."

Javert seemed to be listening. He looked at Marius and said to himself, "This man was in the barricade... This is the one they called Marius."

■feed into ～に流れ込む ■pour ~ onto ～を…に注ぐ ■feel a presence 気配を感じる ■grab ~ by the shoulders ～の肩を掴む

188   Part V: Jean Valjean

III

　二人は外にたどり着いた。ジャン・ヴァルジャンの足元には小川があり、その水は下水に流れ込んでいた。ジャン・ヴァルジャンは小川の前にかがみ、マリウスを下ろし、水を手ですくってマリウスの顔に注いだ。こうしているうちに、誰かが自分に近づく気配を感じた。見上げてみると、ジャヴェールだった！

　ジャヴェールは「ジャン・ヴァルジャン」と険しい声で言い、かつての罪人の肩をつかんだ。

　「ジャヴェール警視」とジャン・ヴァルジャンは言った。「私はあなたの囚人です。昨晩住所をお知らせしたのは、仮に私が生き長らえたとして、あなたが私のことを見つけられるようにと思ってのことです。連行されてもかまいませんが、一つお力を貸していただけないでしょうか。この瀕死の若者を、祖父の家へと連れていくのを手伝っていただきたいのです」

　ジャヴェールは耳を傾けている様子だった。マリウスを見て、「この男はバリケードにいたな。マリウスと呼ばれていた男だ」と独りごちた。

ジャン・ヴァルジャン　189

Javert looked at Jean Valjean.

"He is wounded," Javert said. "You brought him here from the barricade?"

"He must go to his grandfather's," said Jean Valjean, and showed him the message in Marius's notebook.

Javert was silent. But a minute later, he was traveling in a hired carriage with the two men to the Rue des Filles du Calvaire.

When they arrived at the grandfather's house, Javert knocked and said in his most official tone, "I must speak to Monsieur Gillenormand. His son has been brought home. He is dead."

These words caused a great stir in the great house. Marius was taken immediately to a bed, a doctor was called, and the grandfather came rushing into the room where Marius lay. Seeing his grandson, Monsieur Gillenormand fell to his knees and wept.

Javert left unnoticed from this scene and returned to his prisoner, Jean Valjean, who was waiting for him in the carriage.

■hired carriage 辻馬車《当時のタクシー》　■official tone 形式ばった口調　■cause a great stir 大騒動を起こす　■fall to one's knees ひざまずく

ジャヴェールはジャン・ヴァルジャンの方を見た。

「この男はけがをしているな」とジャヴェールは言った。「お前がバリケードからここまで運んできたのか」

「この人は祖父の所に行かなければならないのです」とジャン・ヴァルジャンは言い、マリウスのノートに書かれたメッセージを見せた。

ジャヴェールは何も言わなかった。しかしその後まもなく、ジャヴェールは二人の男とともに辻馬車でフィーユ・デュ・カルヴェール通りへ向かっていた。

祖父の家に着くと、ジャヴェールは扉をノックし、いかにも形式ばった口調で言った。「ムッシュ・ジルノルマンにお話があります。息子さんを家にお連れしました。お亡くなりです」

この言葉に邸宅中が上を下への大騒ぎとなった。マリウスは直ちにベッドへと運ばれて、医者が呼ばれた。祖父はマリウスが横たわっている部屋へと駆けつけた。孫を見るなり、ムッシュ・ジルノルマンはひざまずいて泣き崩れた。

ジャヴェールはこの場を誰にも知られずに去り、馬車の中で帰りを待ち受けていた囚人、ジャン・ヴァルジャンの下へと戻った。

"Inspector Javert," said Jean Valjean, "please allow me to go home to say good bye. Then do with me what you will."

Javert was silent for a moment. Then he nodded and told the driver, "Go to 7, Rue de l'Homme Armé!"

When they reached Jean Valjean's house, they both exited the carriage.

"Very well," said Javert roughly. "Go up. I will wait here."

Jean Valjean turned and entered his house. He went up the stairs. When he reached the landing, he looked out the window, and his eyes grew wide at what he saw—or rather, what he didn't see.

Javert was gone.

■do with ～を処置する ■landing 图階段の踊り場 ■eyes grow wide 目を見開く
■or rather むしろ厳密に言えば

「ジャヴェール警視」とジャン・ヴァルジャンは言った。「自宅に帰り、別れを告げさせてください。それから、どうぞあなたの仕事をなさってください」

ジャヴェールはしばし無言だった。それからうなずき、御者に「ロム・アルメ通り７番地へ行ってくれ」と命じた。

ジャン・ヴァルジャンの家に着くと、二人は馬車から外に出た。

「結構」とジャヴェールはぶっきらぼうに言った。「行くがいい。ここで待っているから」

ジャン・ヴァルジャンは踵を返し、自宅に入って階段を上がった。踊り場に着き、窓から外を眺めた。その時目にしたもの、いや、目にしなかったものに、ジャン・ヴァルジャンは目を見張った。

ジャヴェールは姿を消していたのだ。

IV

Slowly, without quite knowing what he was doing, Javert had turned and walked away from the Rue de l'Homme Armé. He walked with his head down, deep in thought. Whether he knew it or not, he was heading toward the Seine River.

Javert had just done something he couldn't comprehend. He had let a prisoner go. But at the same time something in him had not let him condemn a man who had saved his life. He felt that Jean Valjean had done him a favor, and according to his principles, he had to repay that favor. But this, he thought, shuddering, put him on the same level as a convict—he owed his life to a convict and he had repaid it by letting the convict go. How could this be? Who was Javert? He searched hard but couldn't find himself anymore.

■with one's head down うなだれて ■whether someone knows or not（人が）知っているかどうか分からない ■do ~ a favor ～のために一肌脱ぐ ■according to one's principles 自分の信念に基づいて ■repay a favor 恩に報いる

IV

　ゆっくり、何をしているのか自分でもわからずに、ジャヴェールは踵を返してロム・アルメ通りから立ち去っていた。頭を垂れて、深く考えに沈んでいた。知ってか知らでか、セーヌ川の方に向かっていた。

　ジャヴェールは自分のとった行動が我ながら理解できなかった。囚人を解き放ったのだ。しかし同時に、ジャヴェールの心の中の何かが、自分の命を救った男を糾弾することを許さなかった。ジャン・ヴァルジャンには恩義がある。自分の行動原理に照らせば、その恩義に報いなければならない。しかし、それでは自分を罪人と同じ所に貶めることになるのではないか。ジャヴェールは、身震いしながらこう考えた。罪人に命を助けられ、その見返りとして、罪人を解き放ったのだ。どうしてこんなことが許されようか。ジャヴェール、お前は何者だ。答えを必死に求めたが、もう自分を見つめることはできなかった。

ジャン・ヴァルジャン　195

Jean Valjean greatly confused him. The convict's generosity overwhelmed him. He thought of him as Mayor Madeleine and all the good deeds he had done. He was a criminal, and yet Javert found himself respecting him. This was horrible; this he could not live with. He felt all the principles that had shaped and guided his life crumble away—they did not mean anything anymore!

By this time Javert had reached the Seine. He stood on a bridge, looking down into the shadows of the water. There were only two ways out of this philosophical problem: Go back to Jean Valjean and return the criminal to prison. Or...

Suddenly, Javert took off his hat and laid it on the railing of the bridge. A moment later, a tall, dark figure could be seen standing on the edge of the bridge, bent toward the Seine. A moment more, and the figure sprang into the darkness. There was a splash, and then there was nothing.

■good deed 善行　■and yet それにもかかわらず　■crumble away 砕け散る
■railing 图手すり　■bend toward ～のほうへ向く　■spring into ～に飛び込む

ジャン・ヴァルジャンによって、ジャヴェールの心は大いにかき乱され
ていた。罪人の寛大な心に気圧されてしまったのだ。ジャヴェールは、マ
ドレーヌ市長としてのジャン・ヴァルジャン、そしてジャン・ヴァルジャ
ンが行ってきた数多の善き行いを振り返ってみた。罪人ではあるが、畏敬
の念を覚えずにはいられなかった。それは、あまりにもおそろしく、耐え
がたい事実だった。これまで自分の人生を築き上げ、導いてきたあらゆる
原理が崩れ落ち、もはや何の意味も持たないように思えてきた。

　そうこうするうちに、ジャヴェールはセーヌ川にたどり着いた。橋の上
に立ち、暗い水面をのぞき込んだ。人生の根本を揺さぶるこの問題を解決
するには、二つの方法しかなかった。一つは、ジャン・ヴァルジャンの下
に戻り、犯罪者を牢屋に戻す。あるいは……

　ジャヴェールはやおら帽子を脱ぎ、橋の手すりの上に置いた。次の瞬間、
背の高い黒影が橋の端に立ち、頭をセーヌ川に向けた。さらに次の瞬間、そ
の人影は暗闇へと飛び込んだ。水しぶきが上がり、後には何も残らなかっ
た。

V

Marius recovered quickly. He was young, he had a good doctor, and luckily, no bullets remained inside him. However, he was still a rebel, and his grandfather was still a royalist. Marius felt that his grandfather was waiting for the right moment to denounce his actions. As he recovered, he prepared for the fight he thought he would have with Monsieur Gillenormand.

What Marius did not realize was that his grandfather loved him more than he loved his politics. Monsieur Gillenormand was so overjoyed to have his grandson alive, safe, and recovering that he had quite forgiven Marius of his revolutionism. All he wanted was for Marius to be healthy again.

With this in mind, one day Monsieur Gillenormand said to Marius, "My dear boy, perhaps it is time for you to eat meat instead of fish. Fried fish is perfect for a man early in his recovery, but meat will put you back on your feet."

■wait for the right moment 頃合を見計らう ■with this in mind この点を考慮して ■put someone back on someone's feet (人を)立ち直らせる

V

　マリウスの回復は早かった。若かったし、よい医者にも恵まれた。さらに幸運なことに、体内に弾丸は残っていなかった。しかし、マリウスは相変わらず反逆者で、祖父は相変わらず王政主義者だった。祖父が自分の行いを糾弾するべく時機を伺っているのではないか、とマリウスは内心思っていた。回復するにつれて、ムッシュ・ジルノルマンとの来るべき戦いに備えて心の準備をした。

　祖父が政治よりもマリウスを愛していることに、マリウスは気付かなかった。ムッシュ・ジルノルマンは、孫が無事に一命をとりとめて回復していることを心から喜び、マリウスの革命思想を許した。ムッシュ・ジルノルマンのただ一つの願いは、マリウスが健康を取り戻すことだけだった。

　こう考えて、ある日ムッシュ・ジルノルマンはマリウスにこう言った。「さあ、魚の代わりに肉を食べてもいい頃だろう。揚げ魚は回復の早い段階の時にはよいが、体をよくするには肉だ」

Marius glared at his grandfather and said, "That leads me to say something to you."

"What is it?"

"I wish to marry."

"Of course!" said his grandfather, laughing. "And you shall!"

Shocked, Marius cried out, "Really, grandfather?"

"Yes, you shall see her tomorrow if you wish!"

Marius saw the love in his grandfather's eyes and realized he had been wrong. The two men embraced. It was a moment that neither man, despite their pride, ever forgot.

■glare at 〜をにらみつける

マリウスは祖父を一瞥してこう言った。「そうおっしゃるなら、お話があります」

「何かな」

「結婚したいのです」

「かまわないよ！」と祖父は笑いながら言った。「結婚すればいい！」

驚いたマリウスは叫んだ。「本当ですか、おじいさん」

「ああ。望むのであれば、明日にでもその女性をおまえの下に来させよう」

マリウスは祖父の目に愛情を見て取り、自分が間違っていたことに気づいた。二人の男たちは抱き合った。どちらの男も、誇りを胸に抱きつつ、わだかまりを捨てた瞬間だった。

VI

The next day Cosette and Jean Valjean visited Marius. The two lovers were overwhelmed with happiness to see each other again. As the old people looked on, Cosette wept with joy while Marius told her of his plans for their future lives together.

From that day on, Cosette and Monsieur Fauchelevent came to visit Marius every day. On one of these days, Monsieur Fauchelevent revealed a secret that astounded everyone.

He brought with him a large bundle under his arm.

"This is Cosette's," he said, as he unwrapped the bundle. Inside were hundreds of hundred-franc notes. "There are six-hundred thousand francs here, and it has been left to Cosette to claim on her wedding day."

■look on ～を見つめる　■tell ~ of ～に…について説明する　■on one of these days そんなある日のこと　■under one's arm 脇の下に　■note 图 紙幣

VI

　翌日、コゼットとジャン・ヴァルジャンがマリウスを訪ねた。二人の恋人たちは、再び会うことができて有頂天だった。老人たちが見守る中、コゼットはうれし泣きし、マリウスはコゼットに、これからどう暮らしていくつもりかを話した。

　その日から、コゼットとムッシュ・フォーシュルヴァンは毎日マリウスのもとを訪れた。ある日、ムッシュ・フォーシュルヴァンはある秘密を打ち明け、皆を驚かせた。

　ムッシュ・フォーシュルヴァンは脇に大きな包みを抱えていた。

　「これはコゼットのものです」と彼は言い、包みをほどいた。中には数十万フランの紙幣が入っていた。「ここに60万フランあります。コゼットが婚礼の日に手にするようにと取っておいたのです」

The reader will doubtless remember that many years ago, on the night of his arrest, Jean Valjean had visited his bank and withdrawn all the money in his account. After his escape from the local jail, Jean Valjean had buried that money somewhere along the way to get Cosette in Montfermeil. This was the money he showed now. To protect Cosette's identity and to keep his own identity a secret, he explained that Cosette was not his daughter but the daughter of another Fauchelevent. Her family was now all dead, and only Cosette remained. She would inherit the Fauchelevent family fortune when she was married. Having been a mayor, Jean Valjean was familiar with all the paperwork this required, and the whole thing was very easy.

Cosette was very sad to discover that Jean Valjean, known to her and to all as Ultimus Fauchelevent, was not her father. At any other time of her life, this would have broken her heart, but at the moment she was filled with joy. She had Marius. The young man came, and the old man faded away. Such is life. She continued, however, to call Monsieur Fauchelevent father.

■doubtless 副 おそらく　■protect someone's identity （人の）身元を保護する　■inherit a fortune 財産を受け継ぐ　■be familiar with ～を熟知している　■fade away だんだんと影が薄くなる

何十年も前、逮捕された夜に、ジャン・ヴァルジャンが銀行に行き、口座から全財産を引き出していたことを、賢明な読者はきっと覚えているはずだ。町の牢屋から脱獄すると、ジャン・ヴァルジャンはモンフェルメイユにいるコゼットを引き取りに行く道すがら、その金を埋めておいた。今ジャン・ヴァルジャンが見せた金はこの時のものである。コゼットの身元を明かさず、自分の出自を秘密にしておくために、ジャン・ヴァルジャンは、コゼットが自分の娘ではなく、フォーシュルヴァン家の別の人の娘だと説明した。コゼットの家族はみな亡くなり、コゼットだけが生き残ったので、結婚する時に、フォーシュルヴァン家の財産を相続することになるというのだ。かつて市長だったジャン・ヴァルジャンは必要な書類作りに精通しており、すべてがうまく運んだ。

　コゼットも皆も、ジャン・ヴァルジャンのことをユルティム・フォーシュルヴァンという名前で呼んでいたが、コゼットは、ユルティム・フォーシュルヴァンが実の父でないことを知って悲しく思った。ほかの時に聞いたのであれば心を痛めたであろうが、今は喜びに満たされていた。マリウスがそばにいるのだ。若者が来ると、老人は消える。これが人生というものだ。それでも、コゼットはムッシュ・フォーシュルヴァンのことを父と呼び続けた。

It was arranged for the couple to live with Monsieur Gillenormand. He insisted on giving them his own room—the finest in the house. He was absolutely taken with Cosette, and he happily busied himself filling the room with nice furniture. The grandfather's library was given to Marius as an attorney's office.

Marius and Cosette were married on February 16, 1833. It was a white, snowy night, and the wedding, blessed as it was by true happiness, was perfect.

The next day, however, filled Marius with shock and dismay.

■insist on ～を強く主張する　■be taken with ～を好ましく思っている　■busy oneself doing かいがいしく～する

二人がムッシュ・ジルノルマンとともに生活する手はずが整えられた。ジルノルマンは、二人に自分の居室を与えると言い張った。家の中で一番よい部屋だ。ジルノルマンはコゼットを溺愛し、部屋をすてきな家具で満たそうとかいがいしく働いた。祖父の書斎はマリウスの弁護士事務室となった。

　マリウスとコゼットは、1833年2月16日に結婚した。白い雪の降る夜で、真の喜びに包まれた婚礼は、申し分のないものだった。

　しかし次の日、マリウスは衝撃を受け、狼狽することとなる。

VII

Jean Valjean woke in his bed on the Rue de l'Homme Armé the day after the wedding knowing what he had to do. He dressed himself slowly, preparing himself for what he would say. He walked to Monsieur Gillenormand's house and asked to see Marius alone.

"Father!" cried Marius when he saw Jean Valjean. He seemed to radiate joy. "What a perfect day we had yesterday! I am glad to see you, but why so early? Surely you wanted some more time in bed after our celebrations last night?"

"I must tell you something," said Jean Valjean, "because you are Cosette's husband and I must not keep the truth from you. My name is Jean Valjean, and I am a criminal."

Jean Valjean explained to Marius that he had been a convict at the galleys in Toulons, and that he had been put there for stealing. Marius listened to it all without moving or making a sound. He stood in complete shock.

■dress oneself 身支度をする　■radiate joy 喜びを発する　■keep a truth from 真実を〜に隠しておく

208　Part V: Jean Valjean

VII

　ジャン・ヴァルジャンは婚礼の日の翌日、ロム・アルメ通りにある自宅
のベッドで目を覚ました。やるべきことを胸に秘めて、ゆっくり服を身に
着け、言うべきことを準備した。ムッシュ・ジルノルマンの家に赴き、マ
リウスと二人きりで会いたいと頼んだ。

　「お父様！」とマリウスはジャン・ヴァルジャンを見るなり叫んだ。喜び
に輝いているようだった。「昨日は最高の一日でした！　お会いできて嬉し
いですが、どうしてこんなに早くにいらしたのですか？　昨晩の祝宴の後
で、もっと長くお休みになりたかったでしょうに」
　「言わなければならないことがあるのです」とジャン・ヴァルジャンは
言った。「あなたはコゼットの夫ですから、真実を隠しておくわけにはいき
ません。私の名前はジャン・ヴァルジャンです。私は罪人なのです」
　ジャン・ヴァルジャンはマリウスに、自分がツーロンの徒刑場で刑に服
していたこと、盗みの罪で収監されていたことを伝えた。マリウスは物音
ひとつ立てずにジャン・ヴァルジャンの話を聞いた。あまりの衝撃に、呆
然と立ち尽くしていた。

ジャン・ヴァルジャン　209

"And so," concluded Jean Valjean, "I do not want to dirty your house, nor do I want to lie to your family. I lied about who I was when I was Cosette's guardian, because it was for Cosette's sake. But now Cosette is married and she is taken care of. Now I cannot lie about who I am, and it is not good for you that I am associated with your family."

He paused.

"But please promise not to tell Cosette. I—I can handle any punishment but that."

Marius promised.

"Now that you know what I am, tell me, do you think Cosette should still see me?"

As a husband, Marius felt a duty to protect his wife. This was his strongest feeling, and he replied, "No, I don't think it would be good for her to have you near."

Jean Valjean dropped his head.

Feeling some pity, Marius added, "But perhaps you can come see her here every evening."

"Yes, thank you," said Jean Valjean with tears of happiness. "I shall come tomorrow."

■for someone's sake（人の）ために　■be associated with ～と関係がある
■handle 動 対処する　■feel a duty to ～しようという義務感を持つ　■feel pity 気の毒に思う

「だから、私はあなたの家を汚したくありません。かといって、あなたの家族に嘘をつきたくもないのです」とジャン・ヴァルジャンは締めくくった。「コゼットの保護者であった時には、本当の自分を偽っていましたが、それはコゼットのためです。でも、コゼットはもう結婚して、養ってくれる人がいます。だからもう、私の身元を偽ることはできませんし、私があなた方の家族と関わりを持つのはよいことではありません」

ジャン・ヴァルジャンは一息ついた。

「でも、どうかコゼットには言わないでください。どんな罰でも受けますが、それだけはご勘弁ください」

マリウスは約束した。

「さあ、私の正体をお知りになった今でも、コゼットは私に会うべきだと思いますか」

夫として、マリウスは妻を守る義務があると感じた。この意志は強く、マリウスはこう答えた。「いいえ。コゼットがあなたの近くにいるのは良くないと思います」

ジャン・ヴァルジャンはうなだれた。

少し哀れに思って、マリウスは付け加えた。「でも、毎晩ここにいらしてコゼットに会ってもかまいませんよ」

「ええ、ありがとうございます」とジャン・ヴァルジャンは言い、うれし涙を流した。「明日伺います」

And so began the daily visits of Jean Valjean. Cosette did not understand why her father would not come to live with her and Marius, and why he did not come visit in the daytime, only in the evenings. She tried to convince him to change his ways, but he always refused, and in the end, Cosette decided to let her father have his way. She did not complain.

For a while, Jean Valjean came every evening. However, gradually, the visits became less frequent, and one day Jean Valjean stopped coming at all. Cosette, though saddened by this, was busy with the engagements of her new life. She thought her father must have his own reasons for not coming, and she did not ask questions.

Jean Valjean had decided not to disturb the happy couple with his presence anymore. Being away from Cosette made him miserable, but he accepted this. It was best for Cosette if he stayed away. So he sat in his room. He soon found he was becoming very weak. If a doctor had seen Jean Valjean, he would have said that he was dying of a broken heart.

■convince ~ to …するよう~を説得する　■at all 少しも（~ない）　■stay away 近寄らないでいる　■die of ~がもとで死ぬ

こうして、ジャン・ヴァルジャンは毎日訪問するようになった。コゼットは、父がなぜ自分やマリウスと一緒に暮らさないのか、なぜ日中ではなく夕方にしかやってこないのかわからなかった。コゼットは父に、やり方を変えるように説得しようとしたが、父はいつも断った。結局、コゼットは父の好きなようにやらせることとして、文句を言わなくなった。

　しばらくの間、ジャン・ヴァルジャンは毎晩やって来た。しかし次第に、訪問はまばらになり、ある日ジャン・ヴァルジャンは来るのを全くやめた。コゼットはこれに悲しんだが、新しい生活でやるべきことで忙しくしていた。父が来ないのは父なりの理由があるのだろうと考えて、あえて理由を聞くことはなかった。

　ジャン・ヴァルジャンは、幸せな二人の前に現れて邪魔をするまいと心に決めていた。コゼットと離れることでみじめに思ったが、つらい現実を受け入れたのだ。自分が離れていることが、コゼットにとっては一番よいはずだ。だから、ジャン・ヴァルジャンは、自分の部屋に座っていた。ほどなく、体がひどく弱ってきたと感じた。もし医者がジャン・ヴァルジャンを診察したら、心痛で命が尽きかけていると見立てたことだろう。

VIII

Meanwhile, although the young people were happy together, Cosette was sad that she didn't see her father, and Marius was troubled by what he knew about Jean Valjean. He tried researching Jean Valjean's past, but all he could find out was that more than ten years ago, he took out six-hundred thousand francs from the account of a Monsieur Madeleine, a popular mayor of Montreuil-sur-Mer. He also remembered the night of the battle of the barricade, when he saw Jean Valjean take the policeman, Javert, outside. He had heard the gun go off. This made him a murderer in addition to a robber, and Marius shuddered at the thought of such a man being near his dear Cosette.

However, all things come to an end, and this portrait of Jean Valjean changed one fateful day.

Marius was in his office when his servant entered to tell him a man had come to see him. It was a man by the name of Thénard. Marius put down his pen.

■go off 発砲する　■murderer 图殺人者　■shudder at the thought of 〜を考える とぞっとする　■come to an end 終わる　■portrait of 〜の肖像

VIII

　一方、若い二人はともに暮らしていたが、コゼットは父に会えず寂しい思いをしており、マリウスは、ジャン・ヴァルジャンの秘密を知って苦しんだ。マリウスはジャン・ヴァルジャンの過去を知ろうとしたが、知りえたことと言えば、10年以上前、モントルイユ＝シュル＝メール市長として人気のあったムッシュ・マドレーヌの口座から60万フランを引き出したという事実だけだった。マリウスはまた、バリケードでの戦いの夜、ジャン・ヴァルジャンがジャヴェールという名の警官を外に連れ出したことを覚えていた。その時、マリウスは銃声を耳にした。これで、ジャン・ヴァルジャンは、盗みに加えて殺人の罪を犯したことになる。マリウスは、そんな男が愛しのコゼットの周りをうろついていると考えただけでも身震いした。

　しかし、すべてが終わりを告げた。ある運命の日、ジャン・ヴァルジャンのイメージは一変したのだ。
　マリウスが事務室に座っていると、召使いがやってきて、ある男が面会を求めてきたと言った。テナールという名の男だった。マリウスはペンを置いた。

ジャン・ヴァルジャン　215

"Tell him to enter."

In came Thénardier. Marius recognized him immediately, but he only said, "How can I help you?"

"Sir, I'm sorry to disturb you. My name is Thénard, and I have some very important information to tell you," he said with a sly look. "It is information that could harm your family. It pertains to your wife's father. Of course, I want to tell you from the goodness of my heart, but you see, I'm a poor man and all I ask is twenty thousand francs in repayment for my information."

Marius stood up.

"I know you," he said. "Your name is really Thénardier. I also know the information you want to tell me. I have no need for you. Please go."

"You don't know this information! The father of your wife is a criminal—a robber and an assassin! I will tell you more if you pay me."

■sly look ずるそうな目つき　■pertain to ～に関連する　■from goodness of one's heart 親切心から　■you see ご存知でしょう

「入るように言いなさい」

　テナルディエが入って来た。マリウスはすぐにわかったが、「どうしましたか」とだけ言った。

　「お邪魔をして申し訳ありません。私の名前はテナールです。とても大切な知らせがあります」テナルディエは狡猾な笑みを浮かべた。「あなたの家族を脅かす可能性のある情報です。奥様のお父様についての話ですよ。もちろん、善意でお伝えするのですが、ご覧の通り私は金に困っておりまして、この情報に２万フランいただければと思っております」

　マリウスは立ち上がった。

　「あなたのことは知っています」とマリウスは言った。「あなたの本名はテナルディエでしょう。あなたの伝えたい情報のことも知っています。あなたと話す必要はありません。どうぞ出て行ってください」

　「この情報はご存じないはずです！　あなたの奥様のお父様は罪人なのです。盗人であり、人殺しです。金をくれたらもっとお話ししますよ」

"Enough! He told me that himself! His name is Jean Valjean, and he escaped from prison. I know he is a robber because he took six hundred thousand francs from a man named Madeleine. He gave it to my wife, but neither she nor I have touched it. It is dirty money. I know he is an assassin because he killed the police officer, Javert."

At this, Thénardier began to smile. He had the look of someone who had just won a game.

"You are wrong, sir," said Thénardier. "Jean Valjean never robbed Monsieur Madeleine because he *was* Monsieur Madeleine. He never killed Javert, because Javert killed himself. I have proof."

Thénardier showed him two old, yellowed newspaper clippings. The first established the identity of Jean Valjean as Monsieur Madeleine. The second was a report on the suicide of police inspector Javert.

"Goodness! Oh!" cried Marius. "Then this man is not a robber but a hero!"

"You are wrong again, sir," said Thénardier. "I have proof of this as well."

■have a look of ～のような表情を浮かべる　■kill oneself 自殺する　■clipping 图 切抜き　■suicide 图 自殺　■goodness 圃 おお神よ

218　Part V: Jean Valjean

「もう十分！　あの人がみずから話してくれた。彼の名はジャン・ヴァルジャンで、脱獄したんだ。マドレーヌという名の男から60万フランを奪った盗人だ。それを妻にくれたが、妻も私もその金には手を付けていない。汚い金だからだ。人殺しだというのも知っている。ジャヴェールという警官を殺したのだ」

　こう聞いて、テナルディエはほくそ笑み、ゲームに勝った男の顔つきになった。

　「それは間違っていますよ」とテナルディエは言った。「ジャン・ヴァルジャンはムッシュ・マドレーヌから金を奪ってはいません。ジャン・ヴァルジャンこそがムッシュ・マドレーヌだったのです。ジャヴェールを殺してもいません。ジャヴェールは自殺したのです。証拠もありますよ」

　テナルディエはマリウスに、古い黄ばんだ新聞記事の切り抜きを見せた。はじめの記事は、ジャン・ヴァルジャンがムッシュ・マドレーヌであることを示していた。二番目の記事は、ジャヴェール警視の自殺を報じていた。

　「何ということだ！　ああ！」とマリウスは叫んだ。「では、この男は盗人ではなく、英雄ではないか！」

　「それも違いますよ」とテナルディエは言った。「これも証拠があります」

With this, he pulled out a strip of cloth from his pocket. Showing it to Marius, Thénardier said, "Because I fell on hard times, I procured the key to a sewer and lived there for several months. It was my only shelter. On June 6, 1832, the day of the battle of the barricade, I saw a man—Jean Valjean—carry through the sewers a young, rich man. The young man was dead! Now, nobody would carry a corpse through the filthy and dangerous sewers unless they meant to hide the body! And nobody would hide a body unless they were responsible for the death! I know, sir, that Jean Valjean must have killed that young man to steal his money! He is a robber and a murderer! Here, I have proof: this strip of cloth came from the young man's coat!"

While Thénardier was talking, Marius was turning white. Ever since his recovery, he had been trying to find the man who had saved him. He remembered being shot by the barricade and a hand grabbing him as he fell. But he remembered nothing else until he awoke in his grandfather's house. The servants could only say that a police officer had delivered him to his grandfather's house, and that there appeared to be another man in the carriage, but nobody had looked closely.

■fall on（困難などに）遭遇する　■procure 動 入手する　■shelter 名（最低限の）すみか　■mean to ～するつもりである　■be responsible for a death 死に関係がある　■appear to ～するように思われる

そして、テナルディエは布の切れ端をポケットから取り出した。マリウスに見せながらテナルディエは言った。「生活が苦しい時がありまして、私は下水道の鍵を手に入れて、下水道で数か月間暮らしていたのです。下水道が唯一の寝床だったのです。1832年6月6日、バリケードでの戦いの日に、男、つまりジャン・ヴァルジャンが、金持ちの若者を下水道で運んでいるのを見ました。その若者は死んでいたのです！　死体を隠す気がなければ、汚く危険な下水道を通って死体を運ぶ人などいません。また、死に関わった者でなければ、死体を隠すわけがありません。だから、ジャン・ヴァルジャンは、金を盗むために若者を殺害したはずです。盗人で人殺しです。これが証拠です。この布切れは、若者の外套から取ったものなんです」

　テナルディエの話を聞いて、マリウスは顔面蒼白になった。けがから回復してからずっと、マリウスは命の恩人を探し続けていた。バリケードで撃たれて、倒れようとするところをつかんでくれた手のことは覚えていたが、その後祖父の家で目覚めるまでの間のことは何も覚えていなかった。召使いたちは、警察がマリウスを祖父の家まで送り届けてくれて、馬車には別の男がいたようだと言ったが、その男を間近で見た者はいなかった。

If Thénardier's story was true, it was Jean Valjean who had saved his life! He had been there, at the barricade, fighting alongside him! He had carried him through the sewer—certainly not for himself, for what did he care if Marius lived or died? No, he had carried him through the sewer and saved his life for Cosette!

Marius rushed to a closet, where he pulled out a dirty coat.

"Thénardier," he said, "look."

Marius exposed the inside of the coat, where a strip of the interior lining was missing. He took the strip from Thénardier and fitted it to the lining: it was a perfect fit.

"I was the young man you saw Jean Valjean carry through the sewer! He did not rob me; he saved my life! Here!"

He stuffed several thousand francs in Thénardier's hand.

"Take this and go! Leave us alone, and let us never see you again!"

Thénardier, who was now the shocked one, took the money and left forever.

"Oh, god!" cried Marius. "Cosette! Cosette! We must see your father now! Hurry!"

■alongside 前 ～の横で　■expose 動 むき出しにする　■fit ～ to ～を…に合わせる
■stuff 動 ～を詰め込む　■leave ～ alone ～を放っておく

222　Part V: Jean Valjean

テナルディエの話が本当なら、ジャン・ヴァルジャンが命を救ってくれたのだ！　ジャン・ヴァルジャンがバリケードにいて、自分の横で戦っていたのだ。ジャン・ヴァルジャンが下水道を通って自分を運んでくれたのだ。きっと、自分のためではあるまい。自分の生死など、ジャン・ヴァルジャンが気にするはずもない。いや、コゼットのために、下水道を伝って自分を運び、命を助けてくれたのだ。

　マリウスは洋服戸棚へと駆け寄って、汚れた外套を引き出した。

　「テナルディエ、見ろ」とマリウスは言った。

　マリウスは外套の内側を見せた。裏地の布切れが欠けている。マリウスはテナルディエから布切れを受け取り、裏地に合わせてみた。ぴったり合わさった。

　「ジャン・ヴァルジャンが担いで下水道を通り抜けた若者は、私だ！　彼は私から金を盗んだのではない。私の命を救ってくれたのだ。さあ！」

　マリウスはテナルディエの手に数千フランを握らせた。

　「これを持って消え失せろ。私たちを放っておいてくれ。もう二度と会うこともあるまい！」

　今度はテナルディエが驚く番だった。テナルディエは金をつかんで、二度と戻ってこなかった。

　「何ということだ」とマリウスは叫んだ。「コゼット！　コゼット！　あなたのお父さんに今すぐ会わなければ。急いで！」

IX

That morning, Jean Valjean had found that he could not get out of bed. His legs would not move. With great effort, he dragged himself out, and he fell on the floor.

"So," he thought, "my time has come. I will die today."

The room was cold, and Jean Valjean did not have the strength to light a fire. It was all he could do to get off the floor and sink into a chair. The thought of dying alone, in this cold room, without seeing Cosette one last time brought tears to his eyes. He had done all he could to repent for his past deeds. He thought of the bishop who had saved him long ago, and he reflected on all the sacrifices he had made to try to be a good man. And for all his sacrifices, he could not have the one thing that mattered to him: to see Cosette again.

"Oh!" he thought. "If I could just see Cosette again, I could die happily...But I fear it is too late..."

■drag oneself out やっとの思いで這い出る　■light a fire 火をつける　■get off the floor 床から立ち上がる　■repent for 〜を悔いる　■matter to 〜にとって重要である

IX

その日の朝、ジャン・ヴァルジャンはベッドから起き上がることができなかった。脚が動かない。力を振り絞って、何とか這い出したが、床に倒れた。

「なるほど、時が来たのか。今日死ぬのだ」とジャン・ヴァルジャンは思った。

部屋は寒く、ジャン・ヴァルジャンには暖炉に火をくべるだけの力がなかった。床から立ち上がっていすに身を沈めるのが精いっぱいだった。最後にコゼットを一目見ることもかなわず、この寒い部屋で一人死んでいくと思うと、目に涙が浮かんだ。過去の行いを償うために、できる限りのことをしてきた。はるか昔に自分のことを救ってくれた司教のことを思い出し、よい人になるために払ってきたあらゆる犠牲を振り返っていた。これほどまでに犠牲を払っても、自分にとって価値のあるただひとつのこと、コゼットに再び会いまみえることは叶わないのだ。

「おお！　コゼットにもう一度会いさえすれば、幸せに死んでいけるのだが…でも、遅すぎたか」

Just then there was a knock on the door.

"Come in," he said weakly.

The door opened. Cosette and Marius appeared.

Cosette rushed into the room.

"Cosette!" cried Jean Valjean, and he rose from his chair in a burst of strength, his arms stretched out and trembling.

Cosette threw herself into his arms.

"Father!" she cried. They sat. There was immense joy in Jean Valjean's eyes.

"Cosette! Is it really you, Cosette? Oh, my God!"

Jean Valjean looked at Marius and said, "And you too, forgive me?"

Then, he added, "Thank you."

"Oh, do not thank me!" cried Marius. "You are the one who should be thanked! You, who saved my life for Cosette's sake, who carried me through battle and through the sewers! You who were a generous and fair mayor! You who saved Javert's life! You who protected Cosette! Oh, Cosette, I owe this man everything, and he is the one who thanks me? He is a saint!"

■throw oneself into ～に飛び込む　■fair 形 公正な　■owe someone everything （人に）ありとあらゆる点でお世話になっている　■saint 名 聖人

226　Part V: Jean Valjean

ちょうどその時、ドアをノックする音が聞こえた。

　「どうぞ」とジャン・ヴァルジャンは弱々しく言った。

　扉が開いた。コゼットとマリウスが現れた。

　コゼットは部屋に駆け込んできた。

　「コゼット！」とジャン・ヴァルジャンは叫んだ。急に力が湧いてきていすから立ち上がった。差し伸べた腕は震えていた。

　コゼットは腕の中に飛び込んだ。

　「お父様！」とコゼットは叫んだ。三人は腰掛けた。ジャン・ヴァルジャンの目には、この上ない喜びが宿った。

　「コゼット！　本当にお前なのか、コゼット。おお、神よ！」

　ジャン・ヴァルジャンは、マリウスを見つめて言った。「あなたもいるのですね。私をお許し下さるのですか」

　そして彼はこう付け加えた。「ありがとうございます」

　「ああ、私に感謝などしないで下さい！」とマリウスは言った。「あなたこそ感謝されるべきなのです。コゼットのために私の命を救い、私を担いで戦いをくぐりぬけ、下水道を抜けて下さったのですから！　寛大で分けへだてのない市長だったのですね！　ジャヴェールの命を救ったのもあなたですね！　コゼットを守ってきたのもあなたでしたね！　ああ、コゼット、私がいるのはすべてこの方のおかげです。どうして、私に感謝しなければならないのでしょう。まさに聖人です！」

"Hush, hush," said Jean Valjean, "why tell all that?"

"But you!" exclaimed Marius, "why did you not tell it? You save people's lives and you hide it from them! You do harm by hiding your good deeds from the world!"

"No, I told the truth."

"Not the whole truth!" replied Marius. "I owed my life to you, why did you not say so?"

"Because I felt that you were right," said Jean Valjean. "It was necessary that I go away. I did not want to bring shame or danger to Cosette, or to you and your family."

"You are her father and mine," said Marius, holding the old man's hand. "You will come and live with us for the rest of your days!"

Jean Valjean smiled.

"That is good, thank you. But soon, I shall not be here," he said, stroking Cosette's hair.

"Oh! His hands are so cold!" said Cosette. "Father, are you sick? Are you suffering?"

"No, no," said Jean Valjean. "I am very happy. Only—"

■hush 圕 しーっ、静かに　■go away どこかへ去る　■bring shame or danger 恥をかかせたり危険な目にあわせたりする　■rest of one's life 残りの人生

「シー、シー」とジャン・ヴァルジャンは言った。「どうしてそんなことを言うのですか」

「でもあなたは！」とマリウスは叫んだ。「どうして言ってくれなかったのですか。みんなの命を救ったのに、救った相手に隠しておくなんて！　あなたの善い行いを世に伝えないなんてひどいですよ」

「いえ、私は本当のことを言いましたよ」

「でも、洗いざらいではありませんでしたよね」とマリウスは答えた。「あなたは私の命の恩人なのです。なぜそうおっしゃらないのですか」

「あなたがおっしゃることが正しいと思ったからです」とジャン・ヴァルジャンは言った。「私は消えなければならなかったのです。コゼットにもあなたにも、あなたの家族にも、恥をかかせたり、危害を及ぼしたりしたくなかったからです」

「あなたは、コゼットの父でもあり、私の父でもあります」とマリウスは言い、老人の手を握った。「天に召される日まで、どうぞ私たちと一緒に暮らしてください」

ジャン・ヴァルジャンはほほえんだ。

「どうもご親切に、ありがとうございます。でもまもなく、私はここからいなくなります」と言い、コゼットの髪をなでた。

「ああ、手がとても冷たいわ」とコゼットは言った。「お父様、ご病気なのですか。苦しいですか」

「いや、いや」とジャン・ヴァルジャンは言った。「私はとても幸せだ。ただ……」

"What?"

"I shall die in a few minutes. But I have something important to tell you. It makes me sad that you have not used your money, Cosette. It is rightfully yours. I earned that money by inventing a cheaper and better way to make bracelets. I will tell you the details to put your minds at rest."

He explained his invention to the couple, and they realized that he had earned every franc.

"Please," said Jean Valjean, "believe me, that money is not stolen; it is yours."

He smiled at them both.

"I love you," he told Cosette, and he kissed her hand. He looked at Marius and said, "I love you too. I believe you make Cosette happy. Please take good care of her."

"Oh, father!" cried Cosette. "You grow so cold! Do you need a priest?"

"I have one," said Jean Valjean.

And, with his finger, he pointed above his head, where he seemed to see someone. Perhaps the good bishop was watching over Jean Valjean after all.

■put someone's mind at rest (人を)安心させる ■take good care of ～を大切にする ■grow cold 冷たくなる ■watch over ～を見守る ■after all やはり、結局

「何かしら」

「私はもうまもなく死ぬ。でも、大事なことを伝えよう。お前がお金に手をつけていないのが悲しいのだ、コゼット。あの金は、お前が正当に受け継ぐ権利がある。私は、ブレスレットを安くよりよい方法で製造する方法を編み出して、あの金を稼いだのだ。お前たちの気持ちが安らぐように、詳しく教えよう」

ジャン・ヴァルジャンは自分の発明を二人に説明し、二人は、ジャン・ヴァルジャンがすべての金を自分で稼いだのだと納得した。

「信じてほしい」とジャン・ヴァルジャンは言った。「あの金は盗んだものではない。お前たちのものだ」

ジャン・ヴァルジャンは二人にほほえんだ。

「愛しているよ」とジャン・ヴァルジャンはコゼットに言い、手にキスをした。それからマリウスに向かって「あなたのことも愛しています。きっとコゼットを幸せにしてくれると信じています。コゼットのことを、どうぞよろしくお願いします」と言った。

「ああ、お父様！」とコゼットは叫んだ。「こんなに冷たくなって！　司祭を呼びましょうか」

「いや、それならもういるよ」とジャン・ヴァルジャンは言った。

彼は頭上を指さした。そこに誰かの姿が見えているかのようだった。たぶん、あの良き司教が、ジャン・ヴァルジャンをずっと見つめていたのだろう。

"Come closer, my children," said Jean Valjean in a whisper. "Cosette, I want you to have my two silver candlesticks. I hope the person who gave them to me is satisfied with me. My children, remember that I am a poor man. I want to be buried with just a stone to mark the spot. Put no name on the stone. That is my wish. And Cosette, you should know your mother's name. It was Fantine. She suffered much and loved you very much. I am going away now, children. Love each other dearly, for that is all that matters in life: to love. I die happy."

Cosette and Marius fell to their knees, choked with tears. They each took one of the old man's hands and held it tightly. Jean Valjean looked up to heaven, and his old hands moved no more.

■mark the spot 目印を置く　■fall to one's knees ひざまずく　■choke with tears 涙にむせる　■hold ~ tightly ～をしっかりと握る

「子供たちよ、近くに来てくれ」とジャン・ヴァルジャンはつぶやいた。「コゼット、お前に銀の燭台を二つあげよう。私にその燭台をくれた人も、きっと私に満足して下さるだろう。子供たちよ。私が貧しい男であることを忘れないでほしい。埋葬する時にはただ石を置いて、場所が分かるようにしておいてくれればいい。石には名前を刻まないでくれ。それが私の願いだ。それからコゼット、お前は母親の名を知るべきだ。ファンティーヌという名前だった。とても苦しみ、そして、お前のことをとても愛していた。子供たちよ、私はもう行かなければならない。お互いに愛し合いなさい。愛することが、人生のすべてだからだ。私は幸せにこの世を去れる」

コゼットとマリウスはひざまずき、むせび泣いた。二人は老人の手を片手ずつ取り、しっかり握りしめた。ジャン・ヴァルジャンは天を見上げた。老いた手は、もう動くことはなかった。

X

In the cemetery of Père Lachaise, near one of the poor neighborhoods of Paris, there is a great yew tree in a lonely corner. Among the grass and the moss, in the shade of the tree, there is a stone. It is not protected from the elements. The air turns it black, the moss turns it green, and the birds stop there to rest. The stone is long enough and narrow enough to cover a man, but it is entirely blank. No name can be read there.

■the elements 風雨などの自然の力　■blank 形 何も書かれていない

X

　パリの貧しい地区にあるペール・ラシェーズ墓地の人気のない角地に、イチイの大木が植わっている。木陰の草や苔の間に、石が据えられている。雨風を避けるものがなく、空気が石を黒く、苔が石を緑に変え、鳥たちが止まって羽を休めている。石は縦横ともちょうど人間一人分ぐらいの大きさだが、何も書かれていない。名前を読み取ることはできない。

確かな読解のための英語表現 [文法]

未来を表すshall（willとの違い）

助動詞shallについては、相手の意志をたずねて、申し出や提案を表す使い方が一般的ですが、それ以外に、物語文によく出てくる特殊用法があります。理解しておくと、登場人物の気持に深く入り込んだ読み方ができるようになります。特にwillとのニュアンスの違いに注意してみましょう。

Go to the trial, Javert, and we shall figure out how to deal with you later. (p.36, 下から10行目)

ジャヴェールさん、裁判にお出かけください。そうすれば、あなたの処遇についてもはっきりするでしょう。

【解説】weの後にshallが使われており、このshallは、話者の意志を表す用法と呼ばれています。ここは、ジャン・ヴァルジャンとされた別人の裁判について、マドレーヌ市長とジャヴェールが会話を交わす場面。翌日の裁判において何が起こるか、ジャヴェールがどうなるのか、それがすべて、ジャン・ヴァルジャン本人である自分の証言によってはっきりする。嘘をつかず、真実を口にすると決めていることを、このshallから読み取ることができます。

I shall not see my child... (p.44, 4行目)

娘に会うことはできない運命なのね……

【解説】このshallは運命・宿命を表し、予言のshallと呼ばれています。ここでは、コゼットに会いたいという願いはついにかなえられないのだと絶望したファンティーヌが、こう一言つぶやいて死んでいくときの台詞です。それが運命なのだ、という気持ちがこのshallにこもっています。

And you shall! (p.200, 5行目)

結婚すればいい！

Yes, you shall see her tomorrow if you wish! (p.200, 下から4行目)

ああ。望むのであれば、明日にでもその女性をおまえの下に来させよう。

【解説】コゼットと結婚したいとマリウスに乞われたムッシュ・ジルノルマンが、あっさりとそれを許す場面です。どちらも、話者（ジルノルマン）の強い意志、すなわちマリウスとコゼットは結婚するのだということをはっきりとマリウスに伝えています。

I shall come tomorrow. (p.210, 一番下)

明日伺います。

【解説】自分の正体をマリウスに打ち明けたジャン・ヴァルジャンですが、マリウスに「コゼットに会いにきてもよい」と言われて、「必ず行く」と喜ぶ気持ちがこのshallに現れています。

But soon, I shall not be here, (p.228, 下から5行目)

でもまもなく、私はここからいなくなります。

I shall die in a few minutes. (p.230, 2行目)

私はもうまもなく死ぬ。

【解説】ジャン・ヴァルジャンが自分の死を悟り、コゼットとマリウスにそれを伝える場面です。ここでshallを使うことで、それが運命であり、避けられないものであることを知っていることが読み取れます。

　この少し前に、朝起きたジャン・ヴァルジャンは "I will die today."（自分は今日死ぬのだ）と口にしています。このwillは単純未来で、未来に起こると予測される事柄を表していることから、ジャン・ヴァルジャンがまずwill dieで自分の死を予測し、それからshall dieで運命を悟ったことがわかります。

237

では、比較のためにもう少しwillの文も見てみましょう。

I cannot live without you. I will die if you go away. (p.130, 8行目)
君がいなければ生きていけません。行ってしまうなら、私は死ぬつもりです。

【解説】第4部、マリウスがコゼットに対し、イングランドに行かないでほしいと懇願するときにwillが使われています。このwillは主語の意志を表すもので、shallではなくwillが使われているため「そうするつもり（だが、実際にそうなるかどうかはわからない）」という言外の意味が汲み取れます。

Just promise me, that you will use this silver to become an honest man. (p.20, 下から2行目)
一つ、約束していただけますか。この銀は、正直者になるために使うことを。

【解説】第1部、司教がジャン・ヴァルジャンに銀の燭台を渡すときにこう言っています。このwillは、主語（ジャン・ヴァルジャン）に対する話者（司教）の希望、依頼を表す表現です。

Blow up the barricade, and you will blow yourself up also!
(p.154, 下から6行目)
バリケードを吹き飛ばしてみろ、お前も吹き飛ぶんだぞ。

【解説】命令文＋andのかたちで「～しなさい、そうすれば…」という意味の文です。火薬に火をつけてバリケードを破壊しようとしているマリウスに「そんなことをすればお前も死ぬぞ」と敵方の兵士が叫んでいます。この構文でよく使われるwillは、未来に起こると予測される事柄を表しています。

　willとくらべると、話者の意志や運命を表すshallのもつ意味が浮かび上がってきます。「絶対そうするぞ」「絶対そうなるのだ」というニュアンスが感じ取れないでしょうか。

238

English Conversational Ability Test
国際英語会話能力検定

● E-CATとは…
英語が話せるようになるためのテストです。インターネットベースで、30分であなたの発話力をチェックします。

www.ecatexam.com

● iTEP®とは…
世界各国の企業、政府機関、アメリカの大学300校以上が、英語能力判定テストとして採用。オンラインによる90分のテストで文法、リーディング、リスニング、ライティング、スピーキングの5技能をスコア化。iTEP®は、留学、就職、海外赴任などに必要な、世界に通用する英語力を総合的に評価する画期的なテストです。

www.itepexamjapan.com

[IBC対訳ライブラリー]
英語で読むレ・ミゼラブル

2016年8月2日　第1刷発行

原著者　　ヴィクトル・ユーゴー

発行者　　浦　晋亮

発行所　　IBCパブリッシング株式会社
　　　　　〒162-0804 東京都新宿区中里町29番3号 菱秀神楽坂ビル9F
　　　　　Tel. 03-3513-4511　Fax. 03-3513-4512
　　　　　www.ibcpub.co.jp

印刷所　　株式会社シナノパブリッシングプレス

© IBC Publishing, Inc. 2016

Printed in Japan

落丁本・乱丁本は、小社宛にお送りください。送料小社負担にてお取り替えいたします。
本書の無断複写（コピー）は著作権法上での例外を除き禁じられています。

ISBN978-4-7946-0422-4